CW00734513

HONG KONG

A pocket guide to the city's best cultural hangouts,
shops, bars and eateries

PENNY WATSON

Hardie Grant
TRAVEL

BEST BAR VIEWS

Felix, Tsim Sha Tsui & West Kowloon … 98

Sevva, Central …

The Legacy House, Tsim Sha Tsui & West Kowloon … 101

Ozone, Tsim Sha Tsui & West Kowloon … 104

Qi – Nine Dragons, Tsim Sha Tsui & West Kowloon … 100

LIVE MUSIC VENUES

Dada Bar & Lounge, Tsim Sha Tsui & West Kowloon … 105

Dark Side, Tsim Sha Tsui & West Kowloon … 101

Foxglove, Central … 19

Adrenalin, Causeway Bay, Happy Valley & Tai Hung … 50

MARKETS

Street Markets, Central … 5

Stanley Market, Hong Kong Island South … 82

Jade Market, Jordan & Beyond … 110

Cat Street Market (Upper Cascar Row), Sheung Wan … 67

Temple Street Night Market, Jordan & Beyond … 114

Kowloon Street Markets, Jordan & Beyond … 111

Wan Chai Street Markets, Wan Chai … 36

SHOPS WITH A LOCAL EDGE

Kapok, Wan Chai … 37

G.O.D., Soho … 29

Vivienne Tam, Soho & Wan Chai … 26 & 40

Shanghai Tang, Central … 8

PRE-LOVED WARES

InBetween, Tai Ping Shan, Sheung Wan … 70

Luddite, Causeway Bay, Happy Valley & Tai Hung … 56

Select 18, Shueng Wan … 68

Vinyl Hero, Sham Shui Po … 123

Hula, Hong Kong Island South … 86

WALKS

Bowen Road, Causeway Bay, Happy Valley & Tai Hung … 58

Dragon's Back Trail, Hong Kong Island South … 81

Family Trail Walk, Lamma Island … 141

Nei Lak Shan Country Trail, Lantau Island … 147

TSING YI ISLAND

荃灣
TSUEN WAN

PRECINCTS

1. Central ... xii
2. Soho ... 24
3. Wan Chai ... 34
4. Causeway Bay, Happy Valley &
   Tai Hang ... 48
5. Sheung Wan ... 64
6. Hong Kong Island South ... 78
7. Tsim Sha Tsui & West Kowloon ... 92
8. Jordan & Beyond ... 106
9. Sham Shui Po ... 118

FIELD TRIPS

10. Macau ... 128
11. Lamma Island ... 138
12. Lantau Island ... 144

LAMMA
ISLAND

West
Lamma
Channel

CHEUNG CHAN
ISLAND

沙田
SHA TIN

黃大仙
WONG TAI SIN

西貢
SAI KUNG

深水埗
SHAM SHUI PO

⑨

九龍城
KOWLOON CITY

觀塘
KWUN TONG

⑧

油尖旺
YAU TSIM MONG

⑦

香港
HONG KONG

⑤

② ①

Victoria Harbour

③ ④

中環
CENTRAL & WESTERN

灣仔
WAN CHAI

東
EASTERN

南
SOUTHERN

⑥

HONG KONG ISLAND

East Lamma Channel

離島
LANDS

CENTRAL

Hong Kong's central business district (CBD), on the north shore of Hong Kong Island, is one of the world's most eye-catching city scapes. Wedged between the steep jungle slopes of Victoria Peak mountain and the shores of Victoria Harbour, its teetering, shiny, glass-and-metal edifices lend a futuristic air to the city, an effect that's pronounced at night when the skyline glitters like a galaxy of stars. Wherever you are, there are magnificent views of the harbour or of sky-high towers, and a tantalising mix of cutting-edge architecture and designer shops with local markets and temples.

At street level, old gardens, churches and heritage buildings survive from British colonial times. Aromatic shrines dot the sloping streets. Street Market vendors (*see* p. 5) sell live seafood, hundred-year-old eggs and antiquities. Against this backdrop is the modern Hongkonger: well-dressed, hardworking and just as easily won over by a bowl of cheap noodles as a Gucci bag.

Famed party hot spot Lan Kwai Fong and, more recently, Wyndham Street, fly the flag for party goers bee-lining it to buzzy bars and raucous pubs, but Central's sloping cobbled streets are also home to more quiet achievers – relaxed eateries, hidden bars and dumpling shops run by old-timers, like Tsim Chai Kee (*see* p. 11). Central's restaurants might be pricey, but they're worthy, especially when dumplings and dim sum are on the table. Splurge at Mott 32 (*see* p. 14) or Duddell's (*see* p. 20) and end the evening on a high at rooftop bar Sevva (*see* p. 18).

The ferry terminals, Mid-Levels Escalator (*see* p. 4), heritage Hong Kong trams (*see* p. 2) and MTR train system make Central an easily accessible starting point for exploring.

→ *Cochrane Street*

SIGHTS
1. Hong Kong trams
2. Mid-Levels Escalator
3. Street Markets

SHOPPING
4. Gao's Foot Massage
5. Lapel
6. Shanghai Tang
7. Vickie Shoes

EATING & DRINKING
8. Tsim Chai Kee
9. Veda
10. Mott 32
11. Brickhouse
12. Sevva
13. Foxglove
14. Duddell's
15. New Punjab Club

1 HONG KONG TRAMS

2118 6338

All aboard the city's loveable 'ding dings', named for the onomatopoeic noise that sings out constantly in heavy traffic. These characteristic two-storey heritage trams trundle a slow-going route east and west along Hong Kong Island's northern coast and have done so since 1904. They're a cheap and reliable commuter transport for many locals, and for visitors they provide a happily slow form of transport all the way from Kennedy Town in the west to Shau Kei Wan in the east. Use them as jump-on, jump-off means of exploring neighbourhoods, including Sheung Wan, Central, Admiralty, Wan Chai, Causeway Bay and, further afield, North Point. Much like the city's loveable star ferries, the trams are crazy cheap at $2.60 a ride. Just make sure you have either an Octopus card (*see* p. 150) or exact change to swipe or drop into the slot on exiting.

POCKET TIP
There's also a tram loop around the racecourse in Happy Valley, the only deviation from the relatively straight line.

2 MID-LEVELS ESCALATOR

Central & Soho
Runs downhill Mon–Sun
6–10am, uphill Mon–Sun
10am–12am
[MAP p. 162 A3]

Responsible for 'one of the coolest commutes in the world' according to CNN, the Mid-Levels Escalator is an 800-metre (2624 feet) covered outdoor commuter mover with a route that begins on Queens Road Central, runs along Cochrane Street and up through Soho to Conduit Road in Mid-Levels. The 25-minute journey (less if you walk while the escalator is moving) is not a single continuous escalator, which is part of its charm. Rather, it combines 20 escalators, three moving footpaths (sidewalks) and various linking footbridges. There are 15 entrances and exits along the route – including a new entry to Tai Kwun Centre for Heritage and Arts (*see* p. 26) – that make for easy jumping on and off points. If it's going in the opposite direction to what you need, take the staircase next to it. Just don't get caught after midnight – the 135 metre (442 feet) elevation makes it a long steep walk to the top.

POCKET TIP

Take a stroll down quirky and cobbled Pottinger Street, known for its souvenirs and decorations and for keeping locals in fancy-dress outfits.

3 STREET MARKETS

Peel, Graham & Gage sts
Mon–Sun 6am–8pm
[MAP p. 164 A1]

Flapping fish, tubs of tofu and mountains of mushrooms: not far from the city's flashiest retail district is an open-air food market that has operated since 1841. Despite government attempts to move them indoors, about 130 fixed-pitch hawkers still ply their trade here, contributing to the vibrant street life that Hong Kong is known for. **Graham Street's** narrow pathway is covered by awnings and lined with stalls selling fruit and vegetables, homemade noodles and so-called 100-year-old eggs. Polystyrene boxes brim with fish and crustaceans on neighbouring **Gage Street**, and on **Peel Street** rice sellers, traditional medicine stores and repair shops jostle for space next to hip cafes and restaurants. Even if you're not buying anything, it's a fascinating look at local life.

4 GAO'S FOOT MASSAGE

Level 17, Silver Fortune Plaza,
1 Wellington St, Lan Kwai Fong
2810 9219
Mon–Sun 9am–12am
[MAP p. 164 C3]

For an authentic foot massage or reflexology session, do your feet a favour and pop by Gao's. It's crowded, especially on the weekend, but it's the real-deal experience. You'll be settled into a recliner, given a warm foot bath, offered some well-thumbed trashy magazines and handed a cup of tea in a colourful Chinese cup with a lid. This last bit is a mark of Gao's unique service, so too is a heated neck-warmer and a sound system emitting bird noises that set the scene for a very local form of relaxation. Don't expect a Western-style beauty treatment – the masseuses, who likely do not speak English, tend to focus on the feet, not the person at the end of them. It can also be a social session for expats and locals who use it as an excuse to catch up. Sessions are usually 50 minutes or 65 minutes ($238/$298) but can go to 125 minutes ($518). While you're at it, get a Shanghai pedi, the one where they shave off all that dead skin.

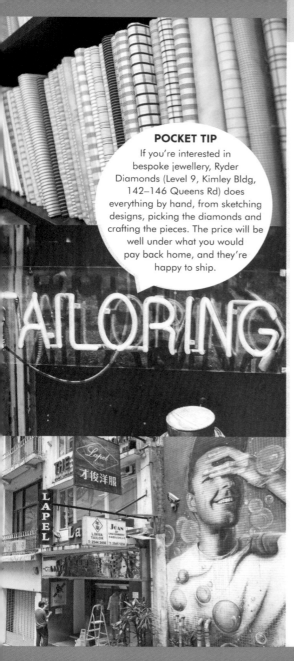

5 LAPEL

2nd floor, 38 Cochrane St
2851 1969
Mon–Sun 10am–8pm
[MAP p. 164 A1]

It can be slightly baffling finding a tailor in Hong Kong, given they all look like carbon copies of each other. Reality check – a lot of the clothes are made in the same factory over the border in China. Armed with this information, look no further than Lapel, a friendly place with a team of gents who will happily measure you up for a stylish classic work shirt or hand-stitched suit and have it back to you almost overnight. Failing that, they'll ship it home and keep your measurements on file for reordering. If you have a favourite shirt that fits to perfection, bring it with you and they'll replicate it with exactitude. The walls are lined with pinstripes and checks in Italian and English fabrics to keep you looking good nine to five. The prices are comparable with other tailors and the quality is excellent.

POCKET TIP

If you're interested in bespoke jewellery, Ryder Diamonds (Level 9, Kimley Bldg, 142–146 Queens Rd) does everything by hand, from sketching designs, picking the diamonds and crafting the pieces. The price will be well under what you would pay back home, and they're happy to ship.

6 ⁄HANGHAI TANG

1 Duddell St
2525 7333
Mon–Sun 10.30am–8pm
[MAP p. 165 D3]

Born and bred in Hong Kong, this global boutique for high-end Chinese-inspired luxury should top your list of retail must-dos. Rents skyrocketed at the original Pedder Street building, so owner Sir David Tang restyled the brand's flagship store with this newer, more glam, four-storey version. Oodles of space, grand ceilings, immaculate staff and the signature ginger lily scent pervade so that the place oozes wealth and sophistication. If your budget allows a splurge, this is the spot for tasteful gifts and keepsakes – the ones you'll want to keep forever: colourful cheongsam Chinese-style dresses, tailored suits, horoscope cufflinks, jewellery boxes, silver-plated chopsticks and beautiful pens. If you're not shopping, just pop in to admire the many gorgeous designs – and the store itself. Duddell's (*see* p. 20) is on the top two floors.

7 VICKIE SHOES

6 Li Yuen St East
2522 9013
Mon–Sat 10.30am–8pm, Sun
11am–7pm
[MAP p. 159 F3]

Here's where shoe dreams are made! Faux croc, fake snake, pleather or leather: if it's cheap, made-to-order shoes you're after then this everyday shop in a market side street is the place to park your peds. Vickie has a great reputation for its 'interpretation' of designer styles and ability to fit them to any foot, big or small (up to size 44 in women's shoes). Choose a style from the shapes and sizes lining the walls, then take a load off while looking through swatch books for colours and materials. Heel heights and trimmings can also be customised. Shoes cost between $300 and $700 and can be picked up within a couple of weeks, or sent home – a reliable service I've taken advantage of.

8 TSIM CHAI KEE

98 Wellington St
2850 6471
Mon–Sun 9am–10pm
[MAP p. 164 A1]

This is a Michelin-recommended wonton shop – praise be. This end of Wellington Street has a reputation for old-school noodle and dumpling joints, all of them cheap and cheerful and with the kind of retro decor you'll love. While Tsim Chai Kee has opted for clean lines and a more contemporary look, it still serves up kick-butt wontons and has earned itself a Michelin recommendation for its effort. It buzzes at lunchtime. Orders are taken from punters lined up outside, who are then ushered onto share tables as stools become available. There's a basic menu with an English translation, but you can't go wrong ordering soup with pork dumplings, fish balls and yellow noodles ($39). Top it with potent chilli sauce and get a side of garlicky steamed greens. It's BYO (buy your own) napkins, which come in the form of a little packet of tissues – quite common in Hong Kong.

9 VEDA

Ovolo Hotel
2 Arbuthnot Rd
3755 3067
Sun–Thurs 6.30am–11pm,
Fri–Sat 6.30am–11pm
[MAP p.164 B3]

A round of applause, please, to this slip of a restaurant that has managed to usher in one of the city's first modern vegetarian diners without any fuss. Don't get me wrong, there are decent vegetarian venues out there. The difference is, Veda's Australian head chef Hetty McKinnon presents it as the new norm. You can sit here and order, say, the gyoza-like Nepalese ricotta and spinach momos followed by a miso ramen and Asian greens without noticing you've gone the seeds and weeds route. Similarly, the baked aloo gobi (cauliflower with crispy potatoes) curry and the soba noodle salad with shredded carrot, ginger and cabbage, feel big, hearty and healthy, with no protein needed. Veda is on the lower level of the Australian–Hong Kong owned Ovolo Hotel, which accounts for its all-Australian wine list (Clare Valley, Adelaide Hills, Mornington Peninsula) and artisanal coffee. The menu humour has an Aussie edge too: 'I love veggies from my head to-ma-toes'.

POCKET TIP
Across Arbuthnot Road, there's a handy little back entrance into Tai Kwun Centre for Heritage and Arts (see p.26).

10 MOTT 32

Basement, Standard Chartered
Bldg, 4–4A Des Voeux Rd
2898 3788
Mon–Sun 12pm–2.30pm &
6–11pm
[MAP p.165 E3]

Named after the famed
Chinese convenience store on
32 Mott Street in New York,
this flash Cantonese restaurant
in an old bank vault is the kind
of interior design extravagance
that Hongkongers love. It
successfully marries the
industrial elements of New
York with echoes of classic
Chinese iconography – wall
paintings, calligraphy brushes
and lampshades. This was
one of the first contemporary
Cantonese restaurants in the
city, and its success has since
been exported to Vancouver
and Las Vegas. The kitchen
has a farm-to-table philosophy
and providence is key to
dishes, including Kurobuta
pork siu mai dumplings with
black truffle and Australian
waygu beef puffs. Deviating
from Cantonese slightly is the
lovely and delicate apple-wood
Peking duck (call the day
before to pre-order). Cocktails
have a local touch, none
more so than the Milk Tram
(vodka, vanilla syrup, almond
milk, green tea, egg white
and cinnamon).

11 BRICKHOUSE

20A D'Aguilar St (via Brick La),
Lan Kwai Fong
Mon–Wed 6pm–2am,
Thurs–Sat 6pm–4am
[MAP p. 164 C3]

That bag stall – yes, that one with the cheapo pleather handbags – slip through it into a little lane that hides one of Hong Kong's coolest urban Mexican joints. Brickhouse takes most people by surprise. The graffiti-covered walls, pumping tunes, mostly male staff (who look like they're out of a skate ad) and covert location work to sensational effect. There are no bookings, so pull up a seat at the bar first for a diabla (jalapeño vodka, raspberries, pomegranate and lemon) and a stick of corn (covered in chilli mayonnaise, lime, grated cheese and coriander). When a table comes up, order the likes of rib-eye tacos with crispy manchego cheese, grilled tomato salsa and coriander; beet fries with Cajun mayonnaise; watermelon salad; and market fish ceviche. Food is served until 11.30pm. Drinks 'til close.

12 SEVVA

Level 25, Prince's Bldg,
10 Chater Rd
2537 1388
Mon–Sat 12pm–late
[MAP p.165 E2]

Beautiful views and beautiful people: Sevva is *the* place for cocktail hour. The playfully colourful interior of this much-loved establishment owes much to the creative flare of its owner, Hongkonger Joyce Wang. It was a hit when it opened 10 years ago, and it continues so after Wang's 2019 renovation. Guests at this moneyed establishment come to eat, drink, ogle the interiors and show off the stunning harbour views: expats bring their parents, wealthy locals bring their families and cashed-up bankers bring their dates. The rest of us holidaymakers can pull up a pew and marvel at the beautiful excess. Couches, throw cushions and amber glowing lights make life comfortable outdoors, where the harbour and the lit-up buildings are the wow factor. Inside has floor-to-ceiling windows, leather poufs and decadent fabrics. Affordable menu options include small plates of sushi and sashimi, mini foie-gras burgers and little mouthful-sized cubes of perfectly grilled eye fillet. Dress code is 'easy glam', and it's pronounced 'savour' not sevva.

POCKET TIP
Sevva overlooks incredible architecture, including the HSBC Building, with its red and green strobes, and, in front of it, the heritage Old Supreme Court building.

13 FOXGLOVE

6 Duddell St
2116 8949
Mon–Thurs 12pm–3pm &
5pm–1am; Fri–Sat 5pm–3am
[MAP p. 165 D4]

Once there were private kitchens – where patrons dined in the casual intimacy of a private home. Now the city has an obsession with venues secreted away behind anonymous doors, in basements and down laneways. Foxglove, a bar with a Cantonese restaurant, is one of the fancier places with the most playful camouflage, but its novelty factor attracts office workers, dating couples and live music fans alike. Styled with a glamourous 1920s jazz-age theme, it is hidden behind a genteel streetfront umbrella shop, which is given credence by its 'established in 1868' sign. Saunter into the shop, then pull on a parasol-cum-lever for a dim sum lunch or a night of live jazz and a meal of crispy deep-fried chicken, Szechuan prawns or baked stuffed crab. Adding to the intrigue, step through red curtains here to enter **Frank's Library**, a den dedicated to rare whiskeys and cognacs, and cocktails with a prohibition theme, such as The Bootlegger, a mix of Old Forester '86 Proof Bourbon with crème de cacao, sherry and grated nutmeg.

POCKET TIP

Between Central and Wan Chai, Admiralty is home to Hong Kong Park, a tropical green space worth strolling through.

14 DUDDELL'S

Levels 3 & 4, Shanghai Tang
Bldg, 1 Duddell St
2525 9191
Mon–Sat 12pm–11pm,
Sun 12pm–10pm
[MAP p. 165 D3]

Secreted away atop Shanghai Tang (*see* p. 8), this two-level Cantonese restaurant is a shrine to exquisite taste. On the lower level, the hush-hush dining room in yellow and white hues delivers fancy meals to an upmarket lunch and dinner crowd; dishes include pan-fried crab claw with caviar, and fried beef cubes with wasabi and soy sauce. Abalone and bird's nest dishes also feature – a nod to tradition. Upstairs it is like stepping into a (very wealthy) friend's salon and library. There's a mix of designer chairs and couches, and an international art collection curated by local artists. Outside, a huge garden deck with pot plants and bamboo furniture sits pretty amid the skyscrapers. It's the perfect place for a margarita made with Chinese five-spice, vanilla tequila, fennel seed, triple sec and grapefruit. Live music and dim sum with free-flowing champagne on Sundays imparts a fun weekend vibe. Bookings are a good idea but walk-ins are accepted.

POCKET TIP

In neighboring Admiralty, the Peak Tram offers a dizzyingly vertical seven-minute, 1.4 kilometre (0.8 miles) ascent through urban jungle to The Peak for a spectacular sweeping vista of Hong Kong Island below and Kowloon beyond.

15 NEW PUNJAB CLUB

34 Wyndham St
2368 1223
Mon–Wed 12pm–2.30pm &
6–10.30pm, Thurs–Fri 12pm–
2.30pm & 6–11pm, Sat–Sun
5–10.30pm
[MAP p. 164 B4]

Among the drink-heavy establishments on Wyndham Street, the green-fronted New Punjab Club stands out as a foodie joint with an equivalent good-times vibe. Inside, the fit-out is uber-theatrical in a post-colonial Pakistan kind of way, with Surrealist artwork taking up serious wall space and waiters looking like they've stepped off a Bollywood set. You'll sit on studded red leather couches at retro timber tables and eat from eclectic Churchill plates from the '60s. An evening here might start with a gin – say a Bombay Sapphire with chillies or a craft gin served with kaffir limes (that are blow-torched by waiters) – then the feast begins. Call it modern, reinvented Pakistan–Indian fusion – whatever – it's really good. Here's a taste: lamb shanks with black cardamom, red lentils with garlic and pickling spices, prawns with burnt garlic chutney and cauliflower with green mango raita.

POCKET TIP
Down a dark alley off 32 Wyndham Street, hipster joint Stockton, styled like a London bar circa 1890, has a wink-wink entry and gin-heavy cocktail list. Look for the lightbulb and the fire escape stairs.

ʃOHO

Soho refers to a groovy grid of steep streets found south of Hollywood Road near Central on Hong Kong Island. The success of this precinct as a lively eating and drinking area is thanks to the relatively low-rise buildings, which give it a village vibe, and the Mid-Levels Escalator (*see* p. 4), the longest outdoor covered escalator system in the world. The bars and cafes are part of the urban scenery on show as the escalator bisects 14 streets. Jumping-off points worthy of exploration in Soho include Elgin and Staunton streets, but in the past few years, beginning with the opening of artisan collective PMQ (*see* p. 28), the fun has started to creep further east towards Sheung Wan. Now Peel and Aberdeen streets attract a cultured crowd, rivalling boisterous drinking spots such as Lan Kwai Fong and Wyndham Street. Hidden bars down nondescript alleys are the new stars in Hong Kong's drinking scene, plus eccentrically glam places like J. Boroski (*see* p. 33) and award-winning The Old Man (*see* p. 32).

Tai Kwun Centre for Heritage and Arts (*see* p. 26) has also opened south of Hollywood Road on the Central–Soho border, bringing new life to an urban block that was covered in scaffolding for near-on a decade.

→ *Street art mixes with street stalls on Elgin Street*

SIGHTS
1. Tai Kwun Centre for Heritage and Arts

SHOPPING
2. PMQ
3. G.O.D.

EATING & DRINKING
4. Chôm Chôm
5. La Cabane Wine Bistro

DRINKING
6. The Old Man
7. J. Boroski

1 TAI KWUN CENTRE FOR HERITAGE AND ARTS

10 Hollywood Rd
3559 2600
10am–11pm
[MAP p. 164 A2]

Tai Kwun translates colloquially as 'big station', as in its heyday it was the Central Police Compound. In 2018, it became the city's Centre for Heritage and Arts, an ambitious 10-year, $3.8 billion vision spectacularly realised. The 16 heritage buildings, including former prison cells and barracks, have been repurposed as theatres, galleries and studios, in addition to two new architectural masterpieces – **JC Cube** performance venue and **JC Contemporary** art space. But the main success is Tai Kwun's styling as an urban lifestyle oasis. Buildings are thoughtfully connected to encourage meandering and open spaces encourage lingering. There are plenty of upmarket shops to browse in, such as **Lock Cha Tea Shop**, **Taschen Books** and **Vivienne Tam**, alongside great eateries, including **The Chinese Library** for Cantonese and upmarket Thai restaurant **Ahaarn**. Have a libation at **Behind Bars** or at **Dragonfly**, with its eye-popping decor and cocktails.

POCKET TIP

Tai Kwun has a Sunday Movie Series of free feature films and shorts. On Mondays and Wednesdays the Lunchtime Series includes stand-up comedy, street performances and mini-concerts.

POCKET TIP

Pick up a 45-minute audio Architecture Walking Guide from the visitor centre to learn how architects Herzog and de Meuron united heritage and contemporary buildings.

PICK UP POINT

PLACE 'N PAY

2 PMQ

35 Aberdeen St
2870 2335
Mon–Sun 7am–11pm
(shops close at 8pm)
[MAP p.158 A3]

Local artisans and craftspeople enjoy a rare gift in this heritage-listed building that opened six years ago as a place they could combine their creative trades with business. Built in 1951 as the Police Married Quarters, the U-shaped, eight-storey double-block building is typical of post-war modern architecture: functional with not that much to endear it, bar porthole windows. But what it lacks in looks it makes up for in soul with 100 or so shops – many of them start-ups – selling everything from jewellery, metalwork and art to homewares, fashion and footwear. It's particularly good for homegrown design shops like **The HK Room** and **HKTDC Design Gallery**, where you can buy unique souvenirs and keepsakes with a local flavour. Excellent eating venues include **Sohofama** for Chinese cuisine with a locally grown bent.

POCKET TIP
Klook's one-hour Central Street Art Tour is a worthy way to get your street art on.

3 G.O.D.

Ground floor, 48 Hollywood Rd
2805 1876
Mon–Sun 11am–9pm
[MAP p.158 B4]

G.O.D. is a Hong Kong born and bred furniture, homewares and gift shop that has taken the meaning of 'local' to new heights. The name is clever: it's both an acronym for Goods of Desire and a phonetic rendition of Cantonese slang for 'to live better'. With a strong design element, G.O.D. takes traditional Hong Kong objects and icons and gives them a modern aesthetic: tenement-house bedspreads, double-happiness Chinese-character umbrellas, market lampshade key chains, panda eye masks, Hong Kong taxi magnets, Chinese poster postcards, Mao badge tote bags, you get the idea. There's also a range of clothes: boxer shorts, T-shirts and cheongsam dresses in quirky fabrics that you're unlikely to find elsewhere. It's the ideal place to buy tasteful and unique gifts for the folks you left at home.

POCKET TIP

The street art on the wall outside G.O.D. is a collaboration between the shop and British artist Alex Croft. It's the city's most Instagrammed site. Join the queue for a selfie.

4 CHÔM CHÔM

58–60 Peel St
2810 0850
Mon–Tues 6pm–late,
Wed–Sun 4pm–late
[MAP p. 158 B4]

Vietnam's bia hoi (fresh beer) street eating culture has been given the Soho makeover here, with French cooking techniques adding that extra je ne sais quoi. The sleek cafe-cum-bar interior on vibey Peel Street has been up-styled with Vietnamese art, ceiling fans and industrial metal windows for a casual-but-classy dining experience. Sit on the front porch for street eating or smell the heady telltale mix of garlic, coriander and chilli in the dining room with an open kitchen. Chef Steven Nguyen's charcoal grill specialties include cha ca Hanoi, which is Vietnamese sole fillet cooked with brown butter, turmeric, shallots, spring onion and fresh dill. The cocktails are on theme: try the Thai-basil-flavoured Pho-jito followed by a Hanoi 75 laced with gin. Or simply roll with a Saigon beer.

5 LA CABANE WINE BISTRO

62 Hollywood Rd
2776 6070
Mon–Sat 12pm–late;
Sun 5pm–12am
[MAP p. 158 B3]

What La Cabane lacks in space it more than makes up for in oh-so-French character. The wooded theme outside, complete with bar for street drinking, continues indoors, where exposed bricks, timber-paling walls, a swing chair suspended from the ceiling and wine-barrel tables take you to the cellar doors of France. The wines here are from small organic vineyards that favour natural processes and are rare and eclectic in a down-to-earth way. Pair a wine, champagne or cider by the glass with pork terrine, beef tartare or fried frogs' legs. Or opt for a fromage platter that might include Roquefort or Comté. The bistro's sister, **Wine Cellar** is at 97 Hollywood Road (on the corner of Shin Hing St).

6 THE OLD MAN

Lower-ground floor,
37 Aberdeen St
2703 1899
Mon–Sat 5pm–2am,
Sun 5pm–12am
[MAP p. 158 A3]

Hemingway, the American novelist and traveller who professed he drank 'to make other people more interesting', is the inspiration behind The Old Man, an idiosyncratic little cocktail bar hidden down a nondescript laneway off Aberdeen Street. The artefacts and mise-en-scene nod to the 1950s Cuban setting in his Pulitzer Prize-winning book *The Old Man and the Sea*, while the palm tree patterned stools, velvet green banquettes, throw pillows and frames give the place feminine charm so that it feels more like a cosy lounge than a cocktail bar. The Old Man nabbed the title of 'Best Bar in Asia 2019' and deservedly so. The eponymous cocktail that pays homage to Hemingway's Garden of Eden, for example, combines rotovap honeydew rye whiskey with goat's milk bourbon, caramelised sauterne cordial and orange-phosphate bitter. Drink up.

7 J. BORO*KI

13 Hollywood Rd (entry via
Ezra's La)
2603 6020
Mon–Sun 6pm–2am
[MAP p.164 A2]

With phrases like 'cocktail
concierge' and 'mixsultant'
being thrown around, you
could be forgiven for feeling
that this is too posh for your
cocktail fix. But I urge against
it. Yes, you need to book online
(www.diningconcepts.com)
but stay with me. Hidden
down a dimly lit back alley, this
exceptional cocktail lounge
is not only for serious spirits
enthusiasts, it's for anyone who
can appreciate interior design
as an artform. The curved
ceiling of the windowless
space is bejewelled with (real)
copper-toned insects (the
work of Australian interiors
wonderkid Ashley Sutton) that
appear pantone-matched to
the hundreds of glistening cut-
glass spirit bottles flickering
by candlelight along the
bar. When you're seated at
a leather-padded bar stool,
a master bartender will go
bespoke on your tastes and
preferences, be they shaken,
stirred, smoked or smashed.
This is an experience, not a
happy hour, so plan to stay
a couple of hours, if not all
night. It's an intimate scene,
so expect small groups, dating
couples and singles with a
glint in their eye. Dress is
cocktail cool.

POCKET TIP

Nearby Iron Fairies, on the
corner of Ezra Lane and
Pottinger Street, is a casual
bar (no need to book) with
a design wow-factor by the
same interior designer
as J. Boroski.

33

WAN CHAI

Once a sleepy Chinese coastal fishing village, Wan Chai, on Hong Kong Island's northern shore, is now one of the busiest commercial hubs in Hong Kong. Its transformation, thanks mostly to huge land reclamation (it once sat harbourside), also makes it one of the most intriguing precincts for visitors. Revel in the cross-section of dilapidated old shophouses, market streets, residential high-rises and behemoth government buildings.

More recently, the restaurant, bar and boutique scene, much of it around Star Street, St Francis Yard and Ship Street, has given Wan Chai another, more contemporary angle. You could splash some cash shopping in gorgeous independent boutiques, such as Kapok (*see* p. 37) and Sarto Lab (*see* p. 38) and those along Sau Wa Fong (*see* p. 39). Then enjoy lunch outdoors at the likes of 22 Ships (*see* p. 42), or spend the evening in a characteristic locally loved bar, such as Tai Lung Fung (*see* p. 47).

→ *Climb the steps to Sau Wa Fong*

SIGHTS
1. Wan Chai Street Markets

SHOPPING
2. Kapok
3. Sarto Lab
4. Sau Wa Fong
5. Kee Wah Bakery and Studio

EATING & DRINKING
6. 22 Ships
7. Bo Innovation
8. Fook Lam Moon
9. Ted's Lookout
10. Tai Lung Fung

1 WAN CHAI STREET MARKETS

Between Queens Rd East & Johnstone Rd
Mon–Sun 11am–7pm
[MAP p. 167 E2]

Wander around the side streets of Wan Chai, between Queens Road East and Johnstone Road, to discover this chaotic grid of pedestrian-only streets, crowded with colourful stalls and awnings. Known as 'Toy Street' to locals, vendors sell everything you never really wanted from cheap factory underwear and clothing to gaudy festive decorations, plastic toys and (often) badly made domestic appliances. But it's the awesome atmosphere rather than the retail that attracts the onlookers. One street is dedicated to butcher shops, the tables teetering with live fish, pig trotters and beef cuts, another is given over to fresh produce with stalls selling pyramids of fresh dragonfruit and bags of nuts. With its entry on Queens Road Central, the adjoining multi-storey undercover Wan Chai Market, where the locals do their grocery shops, is another intriguing insight to the city's food culture.

2 KAPOK

8 Sun St
2520 0114
Mon–Sat 11am–8pm,
Sun 11am–6pm
[MAP p. 166 B2]

Kapok is a beautiful boutique that sits in a quiet leafy pocket of Wan Chai, just up the hill from Queens Road East. Those keen to explore the backstreets and laneways of this funky but understated little part of Wan Chai will soon find the store and be rewarded. This two-storey clean-lined white building pays homage to design with a curated line-up of bespoke pieces. Scan the blonde wood shelves to find hand-stitched bags and wallets, fragrances and homewares, sunglasses and dapper white trainers, plus pottery plates and dishes, handcreams, candles and other gifts and loveables. The fashion lines are similarly covetable. Pick up a Maison Kitsune Parisienne sweater and pair it with, say, a Saint James striped tee, high-waisted crop pants and some classic Saltwater slides.

3 SARTO LAB

6 St Francis Yard
2368 2482
Tues–Sat 11am–7.30pm
[MAP p. 166 B2]

For a dapper suit or tuxedo that will cut a fine figure at weddings and special events forever after, Sarto Lab is the go. From the Spanish tiled floor and ceiling-high wooden shelves to the spot-lit counters, this sartorial boutique is an ode to good taste. Tailoring and craftsmanship is the specialty here, and they're adept at giving a traditional suit or pant-shirt combo a modern edge, be it in the form of a cheeky pin stripe, a striking lapel pin, a cool cuff or a colourful belt. The store also stocks leather boots, stylish backpacks, swoon-worthy ties and men's bracelets and bangles, so you can complete the look. Make an appointment for the bespoke tailoring experience and expect to pay for quality. Sarto Lab will also ship home.

POCKET TIP
Around the corner at 4 St Francis Street, pull up a bar stool at Francis, an animated bar and eatery serving Middle Eastern food and old and new wine to a spirited crowd.

4 SAU WA FONG

Sau Wa Fong St
[MAP p. 166 B3]

If St Francis Yard and Sun and Star streets tap into a yearning for boutique shops, keep walking east (you'll see multi-coloured steps on St Francis Yard) to neighbouring Sau Wa Fong street for more of the same. The u-shaped street, still largely unknown, is a breath of fresh air. This shopping cluster, at the bottom of low-rise residential buildings, is an anomaly, with no traffic save for ambling pedestrians and the odd cat. The shops tend to have an endearing curiosity about them. Behind a chic timber shopfront, **Incredibles** is a small minimalist fashion house featuring just two or three lines of denim jackets, grey polo shirts and tailored shirts. Interior-design store **Lala Curio** sells insect plates, brass animal heads and harlequin sideboards. **Jouer Atelier's** mini macarons come in local flavours, including Hong Kong milk tea and Chinese vinegar and ginger. **Hair House Barbershop** has just the right amount of retro cool.

5 KEE WAH BAKERY AND STUDIO

188 Queens Rd East
2343 8106
Tues–Fri 1–10pm,
Sat–Sun 10am–7pm
[MAP p.167 D3]

For a taste of traditional Hong Kong, this bakery and cooking studio hits the sweet spot. With 68 stores around Hong Kong, Kee Wah isn't hard to find, but the 82-year-old company headquarters is the one to beeline too. Newly situated in a restored four-storey tong lau (tenement) building, the ground floor has a friendly Cantonese baked goods shop. Riffing off the neighbourhood's history as a wedding retail strip, you can admire red and yellow Chinese bridal cakes in flavours such as lotus seed paste and Chinese ham, and pick up a box of signature wife cakes – sesame covered delicacies that taste sensational.

On the upper floors, there's a tearoom with original 1930s mosaic floors, glass-panelled doors and cane furniture, but the main attraction is the new dedicated cooking studio. Wannabe bakers can don an apron, flour the bench top and, with the help of a qualified chef, whip up Chinese egg tarts, pineapple buns and wife cakes. Book online (www.keewah.com).

POCKET TIP

East along Queens Road East, Lee Tung Avenue is a new shopping strip, including loveable offerings Vivienne Tam, Gong Fu Teahouse and Mrs B's Cakery.

6 22 SHIPS

22 Ship St
2555 0722
Mon–Sat 12pm–11pm,
Sun 12pm–10pm
[MAP p. 166 C3]

Before 22 Ships opened its uber-cool doors, Ship Street was a foodie haunt for only those in the know. But the area has transformed and now rocks a name as one of the city's best eating areas. This 'bar de tapa', with a central kitchen and bar stools positioned so that customers can oversee the food prepping, is one of a dozen or so places here primed for delivering food of an international standard. The menu proffers creative takes on Spanish ingredients: Iberico pork and foie-gras hamburgers; jamon, manchego cheese and truffle toasties; and goat's cheese ice-cream for dessert. In true southern Spanish style, this place has a list of sherries, including a drop or two sourced from the famed El Bulli cellar in Spain. There're al fresco tables along the footpath. To nab one, arrive early and avoid the post-work queue.

POCKET TIP
22 Ships' sister Spanish bar Ham & Sherry is at 1–7 Ship Street. Slip into the side door for a cocktail in the Back Bar.

7 BO INNOVATION

Shop 13, level 2, J Residence,
60 Johnston Rd (lift entrance
18 Ship St)
2850 8371
Mon–Fri 12pm–3pm & 6pm–
12am, Sat 6pm–12am
[MAP p. 166 C2]

Hong Kong's answer to Heston Blumenthal is Alvin Leung, a big personality chef who went from Canada's *MasterChef* to heading up a new wave of Chinese cuisine. In his funky duck-egg blue restaurant with exposed brass fittings, he gives new life to traditional Chinese food by incorporating non-Chinese ingredients into centuries-old recipes. His rock'n'roll reputation and the restaurant's three Michelin stars gives the place extra dynamism, but the food speaks for itself. Takes on Cantonese favourites include molecular xiao long bao (soup dumplings) and taro nest made from smoked quail eggs topped with caviar. A seat at the chef's table for the 'I love HK' menu is worth the money ($1380) – it's akin to an edible history lesson. If you get this far, you should lash out and opt for wine pairing – another memorable taste sensation.

POCKET TIP
Few places in Hong Kong retain the character of colonial times, but the facade of The Pawn (62 Johnstone St) in an old-style, four-abreast shophouse is true to the past. A drink or a meal on the balcony, while trams rattle past like they have done for over a century, is a Hong Kong must.

8 FOOK LAM MOON

35–45 Johnston Rd
2866 0663
Mon–Sun 11.30am–3pm &
6–11pm
[MAP p. 166 C2]

If it's traditional Cantonese gastronomy you're after, the Chui family restaurant, opened in 1972, is where it's still at to this day. Here you can try: whelk (a saltwater mollusc), shark fin (perish the thought), bird's nest (the saliva of a bird that's much like a swallow) and abalone (got to try it once). Keep in mind that these traditional Cantonese delicacies are increasingly considered ethically iffy, even in Hong Kong. This four-storey place with the requisite round tables, chandeliers, carved wooden panels and serious staff is the self-professed restaurant for the city's elite. Tycoons, politicians and celebrities front up here to spend big money on the luxurious ingredients, of which millions of dollars' worth are said to be in stock at any one time. For the rest of us, it's the place for equally traditional dishes at reasonable prices, including chargrilled crispy pork belly, roast chicken and eleven different versions of fried rice.

9 TED'S LOOKOUT

Moonful Crt, 17A Moon St
2520 0076
Mon–Sun 12pm–11pm
[MAP p. 166 B2]

There is no Ted, nor is there a lookout. In fact, the enclosed nature of this tucked-away urban bar shrouded by tropical trees is part of its intimate appeal. The look is industrial chic, with rusted-metal window frames and concrete walls softened by retro cinema seats, bentwood stools, white bar tiles and miners' lanterns set to dim. Stack-your-own burgers (with options including bacon, blue cheese and jalapeno) are the go for lunch. Later in the day, try global bar favourites, such as caesar salad, cajun potato wedges, buffalo wings and fish tacos. With a limited wine list, this is the place for spirits and cocktails, such as the white rum and raspberry Red Teddy or Saigon Lookout with gin, kaffir lime, lemongrass and coconut water.

POCKET TIP
Take a stroll around Sun, Moon and Star streets – this block has become popular for cool little eateries and independent shops away from the hustle and bustle.

10 TAI LUNG FUNG

5 Hing Wan St
2572 0055
Mon–Sat 12pm–2am
[MAP p. 167 F4]

Welcome to Hong Kong circa 1960. This friendly, low-key bar at the bottom of an old tong lau (tenement) building, playfully pays homage to a bygone era. The retro fit-out – best viewed at night – starts with Chinese lanterns and a pink neon-lit street sign. Indoors, it's similarly moody, low-lit with plastic light shades and adorned with retro curiosities: old newspaper clippings, oversized papier-mâché Chinese opera masks, clocks stuck in time and vintage public-service posters. The small tiled bar has stools where Cantonese locals and expats alike indulge in, say, TLF signature cocktails made with home-brewed Puer whisky, osmanthus (a native woodland shrub) and lemongrass liqueurs. There are four or five beers on tap. Buy-one-get-one free drink deals are common.

POCKET TIP

Above Tai Lung Fung is Wan Chai Visual Archive art space. Around the corner is the gorgeous Blue House heritage building, which hosts a 'living museum' where the city's history and cultural stories are told through events and exhibitions.

47

CAUSEWAY BAY, HAPPY VALLEY & TAI HANG

This trio of suburbs on Hong Kong Island all sit within a pleasant 10 to 20-minute walk from each other, but they offer happily diverse and unique city experiences. The loudest of which is in Causeway Bay, where money doesn't burn a hole in your pocket for long. This excessively built-up suburb is a shopper's paradise, a neon-lit, pedestrian-heavy hub with every inch dedicated if not to materialism then certainly commercialism. It caters to all budgets and desires, with luxury mega malls, mid-range department stores, street markets, wet markets and one-off shops selling clothes, shoes, electronics, computers, skincare products, you name it.

Causeway Bay's southern neighbour, Happy Valley, is a more peaceful neighbourhood. Known in Cantonese as Pow Ma Dai (horserace place), this residential enclave is famed for its racecourse (see p. 50) and associated high-spirited festivities. The unique green space, looped by a tram track, hams up the village atmosphere. As does the main thoroughfare, Sing Woo Road, which boasts Cantonese gems including Dim Sum (see p. 58).

Over Morrison Hill, Tai Hang is a different – and quieter – scene again. Once the stronghold of garages and car repairers, this clutch of characteristic (relatively) low-rise buildings has been reborn as a nocturnal hangout (it's best after 3pm). Youthful shops tend to come and go here, but stalwarts like Papabubble (see p. 52) and Luddite (see p. 56) can still be found. Cool, independent eateries and small bars, many of them with pavement seating, remain a hit for those seeking more chill than thrill. Craft beer venue Second Draft (see p. 57) hints at a new wave of openings bound to impress the hipster crowd.

→ *Lin Fa Kung temple in Tai Hang*

SIGHTS
1. Happy Valley Races

SHOPPING
2. Papabubble
3. Loveramics
4. Paterson, Kingston & Cleveland Streets
5. Luddite

EATING & DRINKING
6. Second Draft
7. Dim Sum
8. 18 Grams
9. Din Tai Fung
10. Under Bridge Spicy Crab Restaurants
11. Little Bao Diner

1 HAPPY VALLEY RACE/

2 Sports Rd (enter via Wong Nai
Chung Rd), Happy Valley
2895 1523
Wed 7–11pm (Sept–June)
[MAP p. 170 B2]

Horseracing is Hong Kong's
only legal form of gambling –
one night's tote here can make
takings at Western race-meets
look like small change. Racing
was introduced as a British
sport here in 1846, and the
city has grown up around the
original 1450-metre track.
Apartment blocks ascend
the neighbourhood's steep
peaks creating a glittering
urban amphitheatre around
the track. On the ground,
older, happy Cantonese locals
armed with racing guides
and wedges of cash head
for the grandstand. For the
younger crowd, it's more
about the adrenaline-charged
atmosphere and socialising.
Entry to the trackside beer
tents is free with a foreign
passport (or a mere $10), or you
can raise the stakes a notch at
Adrenalin (entry from $390),
a bar and (slightly cheesy) live-
music venue in the pavilion
overlooking the track. The
races are on every Wednesday
night during the season.

POCKET TIP
For a pre-race drink,
The Jockey is a bar on the
corner of Wong Nai Chung
and Sing Woo roads. For
a cheap pre-race nosh-up,
Sheung Kee is a Cantonese
food court above the
Sing Woo Road
wet markets.

2 PAPABUBBLE

Shop 1, 34 Tung Lo Wan Rd,
Tai Hang
2367 4807
Mon–Sun 10am–8pm
[MAP p. 169 E3]

They call themselves 'caramel artisans' but 'boiled sweets artisans' works too. Either way, this Spanish franchise bordering Tai Hang and Causeway Bay is the only one of its kind in Hong Kong and is the love child of friendly owner Ammy Ho. Pop in for a little bag of suckable souvenirs or through perspex screens you can watch staff roll great wads of colourful caramel goo into the shape of the sweets. There are myriad flavours and designs. Some come with 'I love HK' written on them, others with the iconic Chinese double happiness character. The sweetest tooth might opt to book into a lollipop class or a rock candy workshop. Both are available taught in English. Book online (www.papabubble.com).

POCKET TIP
The dramatic Tai Hang Fire Dragon Dance is enacted on Tai Hang's streets at night during the mid-autumn festival in September. It's incredible and well worth seeing if you're in the city then.

POCKET TIP
There are also Loveramics
stores at Tai Kwun Centre
For Heritage and Arts
(see p. 26) in Soho and
in Repulse Bay, where
you can partake in a
ceramic workshop.

3 LOVERAMIC**S**

97 Leighton Rd, Causeway Bay
2915 8018
Sun–Thurs 11am–9pm,
Fri–Sat 11am–10pm
[MAP p. 168 C4]

'I love ceramics' – you just
don't hear that enough. This
squeakily modern Hong
Kong–born boutique is a
temple to ceramic tableware
your grandma didn't have.
The designers are universal,
all artfully chosen for their
craftsmanship, creativity, East–
West aesthetic and practical
edge. Cups, saucers, soy-sauce
bowls and soup spoons in the
Flutter collection are inspired
by classic Chinese hua
niao (flower bird) paintings.
The Made in China brand
continues the irony with its
'big plate' plates and 'very
small bowl' bowls. We Love
Mugs has a trio of quirky mugs
sporting Hong Kong drinks,
breakfast staples and street
foods. Rice bowls by A Curious
Toile featuring whimsical
quintessential English scenery
make the perfect cross-cultural
gift. Loveramics also sells
kitchenware, specialty tea
and coffee-making goods and
everyday items like drinking
glasses. You'll likely leave with
a gift-to-self, and maybe one
for a lucky friend.

4 PATERSON, KINGSTON & CLEVELAND STREETS

Causeway Bay
Mon–Sun 12–10pm
[MAP p.168 C2]

If you're a hip young thing with cash to spare, then you'll gravitate to this (relatively) quiet block, where malls give way to uber-cool street-level shopping. The surplus of Japanese fashion brands, including **Yohji Yamamoto**, **Tsumori Chisato** and **Public Tokyo**, differentiate this fashion hub from others in Hong Kong, as do lesser-franchised names, like **A.P.C.** and **Isabel Marant**. High-end labels, including **Max Mara**, mingle with edgier **Zadig & Voltaire**, **Vivienne Westwood**, **American Vintage**, **Guess**, **D-Mop**, **Miss Sixty**, **Killah** and **Diesel**. Good-looking French fashion house brands **Maison Kitsune** and **Agnès B** are here, or go Italian-style at **MSGM** and **Marcelo Burlon**. Shoe fetishists can check out **Camper** and also **Shine** for ridiculously cool trainers.

POCKET TIP
Two of Causeway Bay's most popular shopping destinations are Sogo department store and Hysan Place, a high-rise mall with bright lights and big-brand names.

5 LUDDITE

Lei Shun Court, Causeway Bay
2870 0422
Mon–Sun 12pm–9pm
[MAP p. 168 C3]

It's rather bizarre finding a
hipster bolthole in dinghy
indoor Lei Shun Court
shopping strip, but it's exciting
when you do. Luddite is a
mostly men's boutique created
and sourced by a Hong Kong
designer with a passion for
American vintage. The low-lit
cosy space is decorated with
wooden fixtures and retro-
phernalia. It's stocked to the
eyeballs with old-school dapper
ware, such as fedoras, belts,
leather loafers with tassels
and bow ties. You can find
Steinbeck-era clothing – check
shirts, bib tops, bandanas,
overalls and waistcoats, along
with airforce-cool bomber
jackets, boots and leather
goods. The owner doubles as
the in-house tailor, creating
old-style new clothes and
giving stock bespoke touches
such as elbow patches. The
hot favourites include two-tone
'50s bowling shoes, denim
berets, retro Hawaiian shirts
and 1930s French worker linen
canvas shoulder bags. Visiting
really is a romp through the
history of fashion. Expect to
pay more than in a second-
hand store, as this is artisan
stuff with a price tag befitting
the creativity put into it.

POCKET TIP
Haven Street, parallel to
Lei Shun Court laneway,
is good for a stroll, with
little bars, eateries, a
hipster barber and a local
fashion shop or two.

6 SECOND DRAFT

Little Tai Hang Hotel
98 Tung Lo Wan Rd, Tai Hang
3899 8888
Mon–Thurs 4pm–1am,
Fri 4pm–2am, Sat 12pm–2pm,
Sun 12pm–1am
[MAP p. 169 F3]

Perfectly matched to the laid-back cool of the neighbourhood, this tasteful residential hotel, Little Tai Hang, boasts the kind of bespoke styling and artisanal detail that big hotels rarely get away with. Rooms have lovely touches like mid-century chairs and throw rugs, but the real crowd-pleaser is celebrity chef May Chow's Second Draft gastropub at the bottom of the building. It serves up 20-something craft brew tap beers, which pair nicely with Chow's spiced-up Asian menu (she's the culinary creator behind Little Bao Diner, *see* p. 62), which includes snacks such as fried chicken with Nam Yu roasted garlic dip and edamame fried with crispy chicken skin. Also in Little Tai Hang hotel, is upmarket drinks bar **Tipsy**, and a quirky street-level exhibition space, accessible from the pavement.

POCKET TIP

In Lin Fa Kung Street, octagonal Lin Fa Kung Temple was built in 1863. It's worth dropping in to see the joss stick shrines, lotus lanterns and intricate dragon murals.

7 DIM SUM

63 Sing Woo Rd, Happy Valley
2834 8893
Mon–Fri 11am–11pm,
Sat–Sun 10.30am–11pm
[MAP p. 170 C3]

It's *Yu Man Fang* to the locals, but if you can't read Cantonese you'll probably recognise it as Dim Sum (these words glow on a green neon sign out the front). Sitting on a nondescript strip towards the top end of Sing Woo Road, this family run restaurant has a colonial-era interior, with high ceilings, fans, wood-carved booths and a menu full of pictures for easy ordering. It's well known for serving 'the art of Chinese titbits', such as dim sum that includes quality har gow (shrimp dumplings) and gin cheun fan (pan-fried rice rolls), available day and night. The a la carte menu has old-school favourites, such as beef with black-bean sauce and sweet-and-sour pork. Adding to the nostalgia, Coca-Cola comes in glass bottles. There's Tsingtao beer, but you'll need to BYO wine.

POCKET TIP
If you want to walk-off a big lunch, Bowen Road Trail starts near here and winds its way back to Central through tropical greenery with scenic city views.

8 18 GRAMS

Unit C, 15 Cannon St,
Causeway Bay
2893 8988
Mon–Sun 8am–8pm
[MAP p. 168 B2]

On the edge of the hustle and bustle at the heart of Causeway Bay, 18 Grams is a teeny-weeny corner establishment, with just four indoor tables, a couple of outdoor stools, a tiny kitchen and a big-mumma espresso machine. When it opened in 2010, it was one of the few places serving Antipodean-style barista coffee (the owner lived in Australia for a bit). There're still doing what they know best, with baristas who have no problems creating latte art with a fern frond, pet cat or love heart (if you're lucky), but they've also gone on-trend with pour-over coffee from Honduras, Ethiopia and Ecuador and cold-brew coffee from Kenya and Costa Rica. The food follows the Antipodean theme. Hitting the spot on weekends (and served all day) is the 'Australian breakfast': avocado on toast with cherry tomatoes and any kind of eggs. Smoked salmon bagels and ham and cheese croissants are also on the menu.

9 DIN TAI FUNG

68 Yee Wo St, Causeway Bay
3160 8998
Mon—Sun 11.30am—10pm
[MAP p.168 C3]

This heavenly dumpling joint from Taipei has gone global for a reason. An oversized glass window at the entry of Din Tai Fung allows guests – local families and expats alike – to keep an eye on the kitchen, where a procession of hatted and scarved kitchen hands slavishly push and prod dumplings before steaming them for exactly three minutes. They're on the table in front of you in seconds. If this doesn't whet your appetite, the menu will. Xiao long bao or soup dumplings are something of an artform here, with variations of the original pork version including crabmeat and black truffle. Don't mind the queues: the huge dining room and swift service mean you won't wait long. Green tea is poured when you take a seat.

10 UNDER BRIDGE SPICY CRAB RESTAURANTS

Cnr Lockhart Rd and Canal Rd
West, Causeway Bay
Mon–Sun 11.30am–3am
[MAP p. 168 A3]

When typhoons hit Hong
Kong in days of yore, fishing
boats would ride out the storm
in Causeway Bay's typhoon
shelter. While the winds roared
and rain poured, the fishermen
would cook and feast on spicy
crab. The shelters have given
way to luxury yachts and party
junks, but the crab culture lives
on in a motley strip of open-all-
hours restaurants. There are
four restaurants – each with
varying decor – that lay claim
to be the original Under Bridge
Spicy Crab. Rest assured that
you can't really go wrong.
Whichever one you opt for, the
ritual is the same: choose your
live critter and wait for it to
emerge from the kitchen piled
high with fried garlic, shallots
and chilli. Plastic gloves are
provided for shelling.

11 LITTLE BAO DINER

Shop H1, ground floor,
9 Kingston St, Fashion Walk,
Causeway Bay
2555 0600
Mon–Sun 11am–11pm
[MAP p. 168 C2]

This cracking Chinese-fusion eatery, with its cutesy, neon-pink cartoon mascot, is the second incarnation of Little Bao, the hit eatery of celebrated chef May Chow, who brought these little buns to the world's attention. The first shop was tiny, this one is double the fun with a bigger menu, larger meals and similarly lengthy nightly queues. The eponymous little bao is a fluffy white bun stuffed with various fillings, such as sweet-soy-braised pork belly with pickled leek and cucumber. Other delectable fusion dishes nod to Japanese and Korean ingredients and include pan-fried short-rib dumplings, steamed Venus clams and Little Bao fries with a scintillating combination of roasted-tomato sambal, Kewpie mayonnaise and coriander on top. The drinks list includes eight craft beers, a sake, two cocktails and a refreshing pomegranate hibiscus iced tea. For dessert? An ice-cream sandwich, of course. Entry is via Gloucester Road.

POCKET TIP

May Chow's craft beer venue, Second Draft (see p. 57), with around 20 beers on tap, is in nearby Tai Hang.

63

ＳHEUNG WAN

Once a quiet residential end of town, Sheung Wan on Hong Kong Island has, in the past decade, stepped into the limelight, becoming the equivalent of hip suburbs the world over (think Melbourne's Fitzroy, London's Shoreditch, New York's Meatpacking District). Bars and eateries such as Ronin (*see* p. 73) and Chachawan (*see* p. 74), boutique shopping strips such as Tai Ping Shan (*see* p. 70) and Gough Street (*see* p. 69) and their affiliated design studios have created an alternative to Central, with a more homemade vibe. For the hipsters in Hong Kong, this is a combination of a working neighbourhood and cocktail headquarters. For visitors, it's a chance to taste-test what the city's trend-forward peeps have to offer.

Adding to the intrigue, the precinct's mess of steeply sloping roads and cobbled laneways are home to pockets of low-rise terraces, vertiginous residential blocks, temples and colonial buildings. It's a great place to get lost.

⇥ *Sheung Wan is a cultural and residential mash-up*

SIGHTS
1. Chinese Medicine & Dried Seafood Streets

SHOPPING
2. Cat Street Market (Upper Lascar Row)
3. Select 18

SHOPPING & EATING
4. Gough Street
5. Tai Ping Shan

EATING & DRINKING
6. Tate Dining Room & Bar
7. Ronin
8. Chachawan
9. 208 Duecento Otto
10. Lung King Heen

1 CHINE/E MEDICINE & DRIED /EAFOOD /TREET/

Wing Lok St and Des Voeux Rd West
Mon–Sun 9.30am–7pm
[MAP p.160 A2]

You likely won't buy anything here, but it's a fascinating look at local life. Deer antlers, skeletal seahorses, sea cucumbers and a selection of dried mushrooms – a la *Alice in Wonderland* – overflow from baskets outside shopfronts on Wing Lok Street, the heart of the traditional Chinese medicine trade. On nearby Des Voeux Road West, the potent smell of salted and dried fish and seafood fills the air (a memorable Hong Kong aroma – for better or for worse). This is the place where locals buy traditional Chinese produce, such as black moss, dried sausage, abalone and shark fins. (Fish maw has replaced controversial shark fin on menus in recent years). The scene here is lovingly local, with housewives doing their shopping and old men talking shop. Don't be afraid to take photos, but keep in mind you will get a better response if you smile and ask first (even if that's by way of pointing to your camera).

POCKET TIP

At 154–8 Wing Lok Street, Yardbird is a cracking Japanese eatery and bar specialising in yakitori (grilled) chicken thigh, skin, neck, wing tip, et cetera.

2 CAT /TREET MARKET (UPPER LA/CAR ROW)

Upper Lascar Row
[MAP p. 160 C3]

A Mao tote bag from G.O.D. (*see* p. 29) is a more representative Hong Kong keepsake these days, but traditionalists looking for old-world accessories and artefacts will love Cat Street Market (also called Upper Lascar Row). Found just off Hollywood Road, this pedestrian-only lane and the surrounding streets are a hub for antique stores, art galleries, curio shops and hawker stalls, selling everything from Mao alarm clocks and lucky arm-waving cats to jade bangles and Buddhist beads. If you're looking for real antiques, sidestep the street stalls. That dusty box of treasures sitting on the footpath is more likely to be off a mainland factory floor than from the Forbidden City.

POCKET TIP
Take some time out at peaceful Man Mo Temple on nearby Hollywood Road. Built in 1847, it's for worshipping two deities: Literature (Man) and War (Mo).

3 / ELECT 18

Ground floor, 14 Tung St
9127 3657
Mon–Wed 12pm–9pm,
Thurs–Sat 12pm–11pm, Sun
12pm–8pm
[MAP p. 160 C3]

Thomas Lee, the owner of this one-off ode to vintage cool, has a knack for dusting away the cobwebs to showcase bygone fashion staples in a sparkling new light. Step inside to see coathangers shrouded in old furs, racks of dresses and skirts, dishevelled mannequin busts dripping with beads and well-loved shoes cluttering the tiled floor. On tables crowded with earrings, sunglasses, wallets and bags, the odd home-decor item gets a look-in: typewriters, cameras, telephones, televisions, lamps and clocks. Aside from the occasional tweed cap, this place mostly caters to the gals, or the gals in your life. And don't expect too much competition – Hongkongers are only now warming to pre-loved wares.

POCKET TIP

The Peak, south of Sheung Wan, is Hong Kong Island's highest point. It's popular for tourists, with retail and food outlets and a viewing platform from where you can see all the way to the New Territories on a clear day. Get there on the Peak Tram (see p. 2).

4 GOUGH STREET

Mon—Sun from 11am
[MAP p.158 A2]

Once the printing sector of Sheung Wan, Gough Street has gone from gritty to groovy and is now the go-to for retail therapy with a design edge. Be sure to explore funky shops, including fastidiously designed beauty shop **Harmay**, home decor gurus **Homeless** and **Home Essentials**, and king of cool Britannia **Timothy Oulton**'s furniture and accessories. For fashion, pop by German brand **Marco Visconti** and exquisite French children's store **Petit Bazaar**. **Shanghai Lane** makes vegetable dumplings on the spot. For awesome beef-brisket noodles, you'll love **Kau Kee**, which still has formica tables, plastic awnings, endless lunchtime queues and cool street art.

POCKET TIP

Detour up Shin Hing, a cute little side street leading to Hollywood Road, where you'll find Japanese 'curation store' Okura, which sells funky clothes and homewares, and men's tailor Prologue.

5 TAI PING /HAN

Tai Ping Shan St
Mon–Sun from 3pm
[MAP p. 160 B3]

One of Hong Kong's oldest neighbourhoods is now its hottest property. Tai Ping Shan, a street with a mix of edgy and ancient, is the pedestrianised backbone of a chilled little residential area with art galleries, independent start-ups and cafes in-situ. The hit list: **Frantzen's Kitchen** serves heavenly Nordic gastronomy, **Yuk Kin** does wicked fried rice and **Craftissimo** is a bolthole for craft beer (sit outside and have one). **InBetween** sells antiques and collectibles with a hint of pop culture, and **Mount Zero** is a tiny bookshop with a cosy reading den upstairs (and a handful of English books). More recently, Tai Ping Shan is attracting higher-spend boutiques, such as Korean fashion brand **Njlidia** and San Francisco-based **Senreve** for Italian bags. Unless you're coming to the street for lunch, don't bother rocking up before 3pm – most shops open in their own time and stay open until late.

POCKET TIP

On nearby Po Yan Street Lomography deals in iconic analog Lomo cameras. On nearby Square Street, Squarestreet is a neat little cafe and unisex boutique that perfects sartorial Scandinavian designs.

6 TATE DINING ROOM & BAR

210 Hollywood Rd
2555 2172
Mon–Sat 7–11pm
[MAP p.160 B3]

Vicky Lau's avant-garde Chinese–French restaurant is one of the city's most talked-about, which stands to reason because Lau does things a bit differently. Her elegant dining room is unashamedly and elegantly female with pink pastel hues, metallic gold touches and bunches of fresh flowers. The cutlery is highly covetable, the glassware sparklingly expensive and the ambience similar to that of a well-heeled beauty spa. Then there's the menu – it's just the one set degustation menu with eight beautifully presented dishes that serenade a particular ingredient. 'Ode to Chinese Yam', on a glass dish with gold trim, has flowers of Ossetra caviar floating atop a pond of sweetcorn soup. 'Ode to Scallion', served on a traditional Chinese dish, is a circle of French blue lobster in a green scallion ginger sauce drizzled with Shaoxing wine foam. Wine pairings are mostly French with the exception of one from Xin Jiang in China. Tate caters to vegetarian and fodmap diets.

POCKET TIP

If you have time, keep walking beyond Sheung Wan into Sai Ying Pun, a similar scene with a new escalator that traverses the steep streets.

7 RONIN

8 On Wo La
2547 5263
Mon–Sat 6pm–12am
[MAP p. 158 B1]

Ronin has a heartbeat that's hard to beat. With only 14 leather-clad bar seats and the rest standing room, this place is fiercely difficult to get into. That said, this curious little Japanese joint, hidden behind an unsigned door, is worth the effort. These guys know food, people and Japan, and have pooled their knowledge to awesome effect. Nippon whisky, sake and beer, playful Japanese cooking techniques and a rare casual ambience make the place hum. A tasting menu might include: yellowtail sashimi, crispy deep-fried scallops, flower crab mixed with mitsuba (a Japanese herb similar to parsley) and creamy uni (sea urchin), and carpaccio Kagoshima beef with maitake mushrooms and a raw egg. It's all delicious. On Wo Lane is off Gough Street (*see* p. 69).

POCKET TIP

If you head downhill to 18 Kau U Fong street, The Chairman is a traditional Cantonese eating institution that continually wins awards and accolades. It's a special occasion place, so go for dinner and be sure to book ahead.

8 CHACHAWAN

206 Hollywood Rd
2549 0020
Mon–Sun 12pm–2.30pm &
6.30–10.30pm
[MAP p. 160 B3]

Wooden stools, a mosaic-tiled floor and Thai illustrations layered on vintage Hong Kong posters add to the good-times vibe at lively Chachawan. Be it a festive lunch or dinner with friends, prepare to tuck into the sweet-salt-sour-spice sensation that is Isaan Thai cuisine, from Thailand's north-east. The charcoal pit-grilled meat dishes here are especially good and are best shared. Try the spicy grilled korubata pork collar salad with shallots, coriander, lime and toasted rice dressing (nam tok moo). Follow it with whole fire-grilled tiger prawns smothered in dry red coconut curry and fresh lime (goong golae). There's a no-reservations policy, which might mean sitting around drinking pomelo smash cocktails until a table comes up. Such is life.

9 208 DUECENTO OTTO

208 Hollywood Rd
2549 0208
Mon–Sat 12pm–12am,
Sun 10am–10pm
[MAP p. 160 B3]

Duecento Otto was one of the early comers to Sheung Wan, bringing with it a New York Meatpacking District-vibe inspired by the two-storey building's former life as a meat warehouse. Here, the interior is industrial steel-meets-wood-crafted ceilings and floors, and evocative European tiles with Chinese motifs. It's a combo that pulls a crowd. Downstairs is abuzz with aperitivi drinkers sipping on apricot bellinis (sparkling wine mixed with fresh juice) and Aperol sprits. Diners are perched casually at high tables indulging in quattro funghi pizzas, salumi (cured meat) platters and burrata cheese flown in fresh from Italy. Upstairs is more intimate, with rustic Italian dishes, such as braised-veal osso buco with saffron risotto, and a Euro-centric wine list with 20 varieties of wine by the glass. Monday to Wednesday, from 6–8pm, 208 Duecento has a 'bottomless pizza and beer' happy hour with seven pizzas to choose from.

10 LUNG KING HEEN

Four Seasons Hotel
8 Finance St
3196 8888
[MAP p. 162 B3]

There's a hierarchy among Hong Kong's dim sum chefs, and Chan Yan Tak sits poised and knowledgeable at the top of it. His high-end domain – the exemplary Cantonese restaurant at Four Seasons Hotel – has been awarded three Michelin stars for more than a decade. Established families, high-rolling businesspeople and celebrating couples crowd this place to enjoy sumptuous Victoria Harbour views in a dining room where chinking glassware and silver oriental dim sum baskets are the norm. The atmosphere is serious, but so is the fare. Don't go home without ordering baked whole abalone puff with diced chicken or steamed lobster and scallop dumplings topped with gold-leaf. This is a celebratory place, so bring a rich uncle or prepare to pay for a quality foodie experience.

POCKET TIP
From the Four Seasons Hotel you can access skyscraping IFC shopping mall. Max the credit card on labels including Georg Jensen, Hugo Boss, Apple Store, Bobbi Brown, Kate Spade, Kiehls … the list goes on.

HONG KONG ISLAND SOUTH

The southern side of Hong Kong Island, accessed via a road tunnel or a hairpin-bend road through tropical greenery, is home to a string of suburbs that are either heavily urbanised or heavenly beach-side. Among the former is broad, sweeping Aberdeen, which combines a mass of residential towers, a sampan-dotted harbour and the road-accessed island of Ap Lei Chau, also known as Aberdeen Island. To its east is Wong Chuk Hang, an enclave of industrial warehouses, home to galleries, shops and eateries.

Head east again and the meandering coastal road leads to the popular weekend destinations of Stanley and Repulse Bay. Known as Chek Chue in Cantonese, Stanley has a seaside ambience perfect for leisurely strolling and a promenade with alfresco eateries looking towards historic Murray House and Blake Pier (*see* p. 80). Stanley Market (*see* p. 82) attracts tourists looking for cheap clothes, bags and souvenirs.

For water-based activity, Repulse Bay is one of the city's most expensive residential areas and somewhat of a beach resort, with a wide sandy beachfront perfect for sandcastles and sun bathing. Keep going past Repulse Bay to the chilled oases of Shek O and Big Wave Bay, where Dragon's Back Trail (*see* p. 81) is the ultimate nature immersion.

Access to this side of the island is via Wong Chuck Hang station on the new South Island MTR Line. Buses also service the area from the north of Hong Kong Island. A taxi will get you here (if you can handle the stomach-churning roads), as will a boat (*see* Murray House and Blake Pier, p. 80).

→ *Beaches are one reason to visit this side of Hong Kong Island*

SIGHTS
1. Murray House & Blake Pier
2. Dragon's Back Trail

SIGHTS & SHOPPING
3. Stanley Market

SHOPPING
4. Mirth
5. Bowerbird
6. Horizon Plaza
7. HULA

EATING & DRINKING
8. Sensory Zero
9. Jumbo
10. Limewood

1 MURRAY HOUSE & BLAKE PIER

Stanley Plaza, 22–23 Carmel Rd, Stanley
[MAP p. 181 B3]

Murray House is the big gorgeous bit of Victorian-era eye-candy that might make you think the rest of Hong Kong looks too damn new. It was originally built in Central in 1844 as a British officer's quarters. To make way for the new Bank of China building, it was moved in 2002, brick by brick, to Stanley, where it now sits, jutting out onto the water like an old dame reminiscing about her long life. There are two restaurants, both of them a little more formal than the nearby promenade counterparts, and the rest of the building is occupied by **H&M** clothing store. A few metres from Murray House, Blake Pier, with its lovely old steel pavilion top (the bottom is a modern construction), was similarly moved from Central (via a stint in Wong Tai Sin) when land between Sheung Wan and Causeway Bay was reclaimed.

POCKET TIP

To arrive at Blake Pier by boat, the Tsui Wah ferry stops on its Aberdeen–Po Toi Island Route. For something more romantic, the Aqua Luna (see p. 95) sails from Central or Tsim Sha Tsui pier south-west to Stanley.

2 DRAGON'S BACK TRAIL

Shek O Country Park, Shek O
[MAP p. 157 E4]

Counter the guilt of excessive dumpling consumption by conquering this popular eight-kilometre (five mile) walking trail. The dirt and concrete trail undulates along a ridge (hence the name) between the hilltops of Wan Cham Shan and Shek O Peak in Shek O Country Park. It starts at To Tei Wan near Shau Kei Wan station and takes two–three hours. It is graded easy, but the 250 or so steps at the start will get the heart pumping early. It's also an exposed track with very little shade, which makes it challenging on hot and humid days. Start early and take lots of water. The flip-side to lack of shade is breathtaking scenery. From up here, mountainous peaks disappear into the distance, oceans meet clouds on a far-off horizon and the occasional glimpse of city skyline is the only reminder that you're actually not far from the metropolis. Towards the end of the trail, the seaside village of Shek O comes into view. This is the place for a well-earned swim, a beachside beer and bowl of noodles before catching a taxi or bus home.

POCKET TIP
Big Wave Bay is another beachside getaway with surfboard shacks, beginner waves and a beachside cafe. It's smaller than Shek O and not as busy.

81

3 STANLEY MARKET

Stanley Main St, Stanley
Mon–Sun 10am–6.30pm
[MAP p.181 B3]

In the mood for hustle, hawking and hyperactivity? This little street market is aimed at tourists, but that doesn't cheapen the experience. Sheltered by old awnings and faded umbrellas, it starts at the roundabout in Stanley Main Street and spreads along a road parallel to the water's edge. The 100-or-so stalls are jam-packed full of hats, bags, clothing, underwear and watches of varying quality. Popular items include imitation big-brand children's clothes and computer accessories, quality linen and Westerner-sized shoes. Did someone say cheap souvenirs? You'll find traditional Chinese fans, silk cheongsams, old Buddhas and jade-esque bangles by the thousands. For something different, perhaps opt for some novelty dim-sum fridge magnets or a very scary Trump facemask. Nearby, a shopping plaza and square is a weekend hangout, especially for families.

POCKET TIP

Stanley Dragon Boat Races and festivities are held in June each year. It's worth visiting if you're in town and up for some fun.

4 MIRTH

3rd floor, Yally Industrial
Centre, 6 Yip Fat St, Wong
Chuk Hang
2553 9811
Mon–Sun 10am–6pm
[MAP p. 179 E1]

A surplus of warehouses
and factories has been the
source of (otherwise bland)
Aberdeen's recent creative
impulses. Mirth was the first
to see the potential in the
wide-open shop spaces hidden
among dozens of characterless
1960s warehouse buildings.
This magical shop (recently
moved so it's closer to the
MTR station), with more than
a hint of whimsy, has a lovely
girlishness about it – not
necessarily pink, just feminine
with a nod to all ages. It sells
all sorts, from wooden kitchen
tables and coloured metal
chairs to Liberty children's
clothing, colourful pens and
pencils, material-covered
stools, ceramics, wooden toys
and finger puppets. There's a
selection of one-off women's
clothes, plus pretty brooches
and earrings to match.

5 BOWERBIRD

Level 8, Horizon Plaza,
2 Lee Wing St, Ap Lei Chau,
Aberdeen
2552 2727
Mon–Sun 10am–8pm
[MAP p. 178 A4]

Australian-born, Hong Kong-based Philippa Haydon has evolved her fondness for blue-and-white Chinoiserie ceramics and Chinese antiques into a full-blow business. Bowerbird is a wholesaler but also sells direct to the public, with global shipping available. While much of the furniture is sourced from New York and Paris, Asian-accented treasures have been artfully incorporated so as to blend with Western-style interiors. Big-ticket items include armoires, bedside tables, dining chairs, rattan and wicker baskets and Chinese-style porcelain garden stools. Luggage-sized pieces include hand-painted dragon porcelain ginger jars and decorative oriental pots and vases. The freestanding Chinese birdcages filled with scented candles and exquisite hand-painted silk flowers are girly delicious.

POCKET TIP
Aberdeen's Ocean Park is easier to get to than Hong Kong's Disneyland. The multi-storey aquarium is excellent, as are the rollercoaster and cable car.

6 HORIZON PLAZA

2 Lee Wing St, Ap Lei Chau,
Aberdeen
Mon–Sun 10am–7pm
[MAP p. 178 A4]

On the road-accessed island of Ap Lei Chau, this pin-thin 25-storey concrete tower is truly a Chinese shopping experience. It's less a plaza, more a mega space given over to furniture, food and brands, avoiding the big rents of the regular shopping strips, so be prepared to hunt. Clothing outlets and warehouses include **Lane Crawford**, **Joyce** (selling Comme des Garçons, Anna Sui and Issey Miyake) and **Bluebell** (selling Paul Smith, Jimmy Choo, Moschino), and straight-up brands ranging from high-end (**Ermenegildo Zegna**, **Hugo Boss**, **Chloe**) to youthful (**Diesel, Kate Spade New York and Juicy Couture**). There's a **Shanghai Tang** (*see* p. 8) here, too. For bespoke reproduction Chinese wares and furniture (that ships) go to **Artura Ficus**, for blue and white ceramics **Bowerbird** (*see* p. 84), and for new furniture crafted from recycled wood, head to **Tree**. Pick up a store directory on the ground floor and – given the elevators are tediously slow – work your way from Tree on the top floor down.

POCKET TIP

Toof Contemporary is nearby in Harbour Industrial Centre (10 Lee Hing St), also home to Artichoke Canteen with a pizza oven and a terrace, and The 8th Estate Winery, Hong Kong's only winery selling tipples from both Australian and French grapes.

7 HULA

5A, Evergreen Industrial
Mansion, 12 Yip Fat St, Wong
Chuk Hang
2544 1511
Mon–Sat 11am–7pm
[MAP p. 179 E1]

Second-hand (or shall we euphemistically say pre-loved) clothes rarely make an appearance in Hong Kong, where shoppers tend to be either brand-conscious big-spenders, or wary of superstitions that say bad luck might be passed along from old clothing. HULA might be a sign that that's changing. This dedicated warehouse space with a fresh lick of white paint and cool concrete floors lays claim to being the city's first pre-owned designer warehouse. Founder Sarah Fung started it as an online platform in 2016 in response to the amount of clothing waste she saw had been produced by the fashion industry. With sustainability as a motivator she opened the warehouse shop in early 2019, with an edit of more than 750 designer brands and more than 5500 unique pieces. Pick up a pair of Christian Louboutin heals, an Isabel Marant jumper, Louis Vuitton dress or Chanel jacket, all for a price-tag well below retail price. It's across from Ovolo Southside Hotel.

POCKET TIP
Gallery stalking? Rossi and Rossi is nearby (3C Yally Industrial Building, 6 Yip Fat St). It promotes contemporary Asian art from Hong Kong and beyond.

8 SENSORY ZERO

One Island South, 2 Heung Yip
Rd, Wong Chuk Hang
Mon–Sun 8am–8pm
[MAP p. 179 E1]

This is one of Hong Kong's best, if underrated caffeine dens. Located directly opposite the MTR station on the ground floor of One Island South, the interior of this warehouse-style cafe is a surprise given the underwhelming urban exterior – such is the intrigue of Wong Chuk Hang. Soaring ceilings with exposed concrete, air-con ducting and plumbing are matched by second-hand chairs and tables that seem genuinely thrown together, rather than curated. The accoutrements of the owner's obvious coffee passion – hessian bags of pre-roasted beans, coffee grinders and boffin wares, plus random storage boxes, play to a functional casual vibe with a purpose. There's consistently excellent barista pours using speciality house blends from the America's and East Africa. There's no table service. You order at the counter and wait for a number to come up on screen, which detracts from the vibe – but with coffee this good, nobody looks too worried. The fare is an East–West mix – think big breakfasts – and daily rice and pasta dishes.

9 JUMBO

Shum Wan Pier Dr, Aberdeen
Harbour, Aberdeen
2553 9111
Mon–Sat 11am–11.30pm, Sun
9am–11.30pm
[MAP p. 178 C2]

No trip to Hong Kong is complete without lunch at Jumbo, a floating restaurant so garishly Chinese it has become one of the city's most loveable icons. The four-storey boat with a pagoda on top is evocative of a heavily ornamented ancient Chinese palace. Local families head here for Cantonese seafood feasts in the fine-dining restaurant. Expats and tourists tend to favour the alfresco Sunday brunch buffets (Asian and Western) at **Top Deck**. The outdoor couches and cushions are perfect for sipping on Aperol spritz and free-flowing champagne. The food is reasonable, but it's the novelty factor that rates. Access is via a short ride from Shum Wan pier in Wong Chuk Hang or from Aberdeen Pier on an old fishing sampan, through a harbour filled with myriad boats.

POCKET TIP

Cyclists love South Island's coastal roads. Wong Chuk Hang's Modern Classic Bicycle Company, (Shop 202, One Island South, 2 Heung Yip Rd) rents quality bikes. Bookings are essential.

10 LIMEWOOD

Shop 103–4, The Pulse,
28 Beach Rd, Repulse Bay
2898 3788
Mon–Sat 12pm–10.30pm,
Sun 12pm–9.30pm
[MAP p. 180 B2]

Riffing off Repulse Bay's
beach resort vibe, Limewood
is a breezy indoor–outdoor
diner at **The Pulse** shopping
centre, which has a string
of beachfront restaurants
taking advantage of the
South China Sea views. The
interior is light and bright,
with whitewashed walls,
throw cushions, industrial
lampshades and long tables
with stools that encourage
mingling over a cocktail
or two. Sticking to theme,
the menu proffers dishes
from tropical destinations,
including South-east Asia,
Hawaii, South America and
the Caribbean, and it works.
Eat pulled chicken tacos with
cabbage, fresh herbs and huli
huli sauce; chicken wings
with Latin spice-rub and
pickled pineapple pickle; or
fried calamari with mango-
curry mayonnaise. From the
drinks list, try summer-themed
rum-, tequila- and gin-based
cocktails that come garnished
with fresh herbs, cucumber
and grilled citrus. Alternatively,
health tipples include turmeric,
wheatgrass and activated
charcoal shots.

POCKET TIP
Also on this strip, Sip
Song is an upbeat Thai
eatery that pulls an excitable
weekend crowd. For upper-
class dining and shops,
head to the Repulse Bay
apartment building, with a
large, angular, feng shui
hole in it.

TSIM SHA TSUI & WEST KOWLOON

Central might be Hong Kong's top dog, but Tsim Sha Tsui, known as TST, is the shih tzu happily yapping at its ankles. Located across Victoria Harbour on the southern tip of Kowloon, TST boasts mid-range shops (along neon-lit Nathan Road) and global luxe brands on every corner. Some of the city's best hotels are here, with spectacular dining experiences, including the stunning new Rosewood Hong Kong (see p. 101), a shimmering 65-storey edifice that has changed the TST skyline forever, and evocative The Peninsula hotel (see p. 98), whose colonial-era opulence still tempts a sophisticated crowd. A trip on an iconic Star Ferry (see p. 94) is one of the city's cheapest joy rides, or catch the serene Aqua Luna sailing junk (see p. 95) around the harbour. In addition, TST has the kind of inner-city horn-honking light-flashing noise and chaos that makes for a good travel buzz.

In neighbouring West Kowloon, changes are also afoot. The West Kowloon Cultural District, which has been evolving – ever so slowly – for the past decade, is now showing signs of life with the opening of Xiqu Centre (see p. 96), an architectural marvel dedicated to Chinese Opera and an architectural marvel. The precinct is also making a name for itself as a transport hub. Across the road from the Xiqu Centre, the striking curved roof of Hong Kong West Kowloon station marks the departure point for Hong Kong's $11 billion high-speed rail to Shenzhen and Guangzhou.

→ *TST's Avenue of Stars boasts impressive city views*

SIGHTS
1. Star Ferries
2. Aqua Luna
3. Xiqu Centre

SIGHTS & EATING
4. The Peninsula
5. ICC

EATING
6. Qi – Nine Dragons
7. The Legacy House
8. Moon Lok Chinese Restaurant

DRINKING
9. Ozone
10. Dada Bar + Lounge

1 STAR FERRIES

Star Ferry Pier, Tsim Sha
Tsui (piers also at Central &
Wan Chai)
2367 7065
Mon–Sun 6.30am–11.30pm
[MAP p. 172 A3]

Famously cheap, authentically
old, endearingly nostalgic –
the Star Ferry service is one
of the city's most-loved icons.
These antique vessels started
crossing the choppy waters
of Victoria Harbour in the
late 1800s, and they're still
going. They serve primarily
as transport for workers
commuting between Tsim Sha
Tsui and Central, and Tsim
Sha Tsui and Wan Chai, but for
a mere $2.70 or $3.70 on the
weekend (it's even cheaper
on the lower deck), you can
be transported back to a time
when slow boat travel was
the norm. The double-decker
ferries, manned by sailor-suited
staff, are open to the elements,
with lovely old reversible
wood-slat seats and polished
metal. Each one-way leg takes
about 10 minutes – just enough
time to take in the boat traffic
on the harbour and view the
immense and crowded city
skyline beyond. For longer
tours, catch the *Shining Star*, a
replica 1920s ferry that does a
loop around the harbour.

POCKET TIP
Time your ferry run for the
spectacular Symphony of Lights,
a colourful light show on both
sides of the harbour, daily from
8pm. Or view it from Kowloon's
Avenue of Stars waterfront
promenade, featuring statues
and handprints of Hong
Kong movie stars.

POCKET TIP

Opt for a 45-minute harbour cruise, a day cruise around the islands, a dim-sum cruise or combine dinner with a city lights cruise.

2 AQUA LUNA

Tsim Sha Tsui (also at Central Pier 9)
2116 8821
[MAP p. 172 B3]

One of Hong Kong's most enduring and emblematic images captures the wind-puffed red sails of the *Aqua Luna* as it glides around Victoria Harbour. This wooden fishing boat, known as a junk, is one of only three traditionally made vessels still plying Victoria Harbour, and it's a vision splendid. The high stern, low bow and curved hull design evokes days of yore, when the fishing industry was at its height and the harbour was full of junks and sampans. Aqua Restaurant Group commissioned the *Aqua Luna* in 2006 and, in 2018, *Aqua Luna II*, a similar vessel with the Ming Dynasty imperial white and blue dragon on its sails, joined it. The vessels are veritable gifts to the city, as they'll likely be the last created with traditional techniques by specialised master shipbuilders. They're made entirely of wood and bamboo, and are fitted like a puzzle without the use of steel nails. Today the vessels are motor-powered and the sails mostly decorative, but it hardly matters, especially when you're sitting on the teak deck with a glass of wine in hand.

95

3 XIQU CENTRE

88 Austin Rd West, Tsim Sha Tsui
2200 0217
Mon–Sun 10am–10.30pm
[MAP p. 174 A4]

The head-turning architecture of Tsim Sha Tsui's latest public development makes it worthy of a visit alone, but if you're a fan of Chinese opera then double the happiness. Xiqu Centre is a Chinese opera complex located on the eastern edge of West Kowloon Culture District (the long-awaited art, entertainment and culture quarter). The warped and wavy exterior, which appears to be covered in metal scales, is inspired by Chinese lanterns, and the sweeping angled entry is designed to resemble curtains opening. Inside, the atrium feels like a public square, with stalls, exhibitions shops and a central pagoda where Chinese theatre performances take place.

The **Grand Theatre** on the eighth storey accommodates 1073 opera fans, but those new to opera should shoot for the 90-minute **Tea Theatre** shows, where audiences are served traditional tea and dim sum during the performance. One-hour multi-media tours, in Cantonese, English and Mandarin, are also available.

POCKET TIP

Try celeb chef Margaret Xu's contemporary takes on Chinese treats at Go Cakes on the Xiqu Centre ground floor. At Mammy Pancake (8–12 Carnarvon Rd), try the egg waffles, a much-loved local sweet street-eat.

4 THE PENINSULA

Salisbury Rd, Tsim Sha Tsui
2920 2888
[MAP p. 172 C3]

Colonial-era decadence doesn't get better than The Peninsula hotel, built in 1928. Stepping into the foyer, with its extravagant staircase, gilt ceilings and string quartet, is to step into history. Most visitors to Hong Kong will find their way here, be it for the eateries, great bars or exclusive shopping arcade (with brands including **Baccarat** cookware, men's tailor **Jimmy Chen**, Taiwanese fashion label **Shiatzy Chen**, style guru **Monocle**, **Piaget** jewellery and watches and **Kent & Curwen** fashion). The dining picks include a lavish traditional high tea served with due aplomb by gloved staff in **The Lobby** – book ahead (www.peninsula.com) and dress up for it. Upstairs, **Spring Moon** is a very special occasion Cantonese restaurant. **Felix** is a sleek little bar with eye-ogling city views and is sundowner heaven.

POCKET TIP

Nearby, is 1881 Heritage, a high-end retail and restaurant hub within the colonial former marine police headquarters. Along the waterfront you'll also find the Hong Kong Museum of Art and Hong Kong Cultural Centre.

POCKET TIP

Kowloon MTR station, at ICC, is on the Tung Lung MTR line, which forms part of the Airport Express line. It has an in-town check-in service for Hong Kong International Airport passengers.

5 ICC

1 Austin Rd, West Kowloon
2730 0800
Mon–Sun 24 hrs
Sky100 Sun–Thurs 10am–9pm,
Fri–Sat 10am–10.30pm
[MAP p. 171 C2]

Hong Kong's tallest building (at 484 metres or 1587 feet; 118 storeys) looms over West Kowloon and can be seen sparkling and shiny from the far-reaches of the city. On floors 102 to 118, the five-star **Ritz-Carlton** hotel is responsible for some flash restaurants and **Ozone**, the world's highest bar (*see* p. 104). On the top floor, the **Sky100** observation deck has a 360-degree bird's-eye view of the city on a clear day (in lesser weather, you'll literally be in the clouds, so check the website (shkp-icc.com). Floor 101 is dedicated to dining, with four restaurants, including the fabulous Japanese **Tenku RyuGin** (book ahead for a window seat at ryugin.com.hk). The Kowloon MTR station complex is at the base of ICC, along with **Elements** mall, which has 40 restaurants, 150 fashion-focused retail outlets, a 1600-seat cinema, ice-skating rink and the **W Hotel**.

6 QI – NINE DRAGONS

Floor 20 & rooftop, Prince
Tower, 12A Peking Rd, Tsim
Sha Tsui
2799 8899
[MAP p. 172 C2]

Chillies bobbing in bowls of
steaming broth and dumplings
doused in fiery red Sichuan
sauce are order of the day at
Michelin-guide recommended
Qi (pronounced chee). With
dragons painted on the walls
and the soft glow of red
lights, it's the go-to for expats
from India, local Cantonese
and anyone else wanting an
authentic taste-bud punch
from the Chinese province of
Sichuan. From the dimly lit
dining room, you'll get a full
view of Hong Kong Island's
night lights, while indulging
in house specialties that run
the full gamut of 'seven' (that's
qi in Mandarin) flavours –
spicy, aromatic, sweet, bitter,
sour, peppery and salty. Opt
for small dishes – mapo tofu,
smashed cucumber, dan
dan noodles and bang bang
wontons, or go hard on braised
Mandarin fish fillet in chilli oil
and ginger or scallion beef.
There's an 'impossible' menu
for vegetarians – respect. The
restaurant has a casual and
youthful vibe, but doll up for
the rooftop deck, which is top-
of-the-pops for trying ginger-
laced yuzu mocktails, Chinese
wine and gin-based gimlets.

7 THE LEGACY HOU/E

Rosewood Hong Kong, Victoria Dockside, 18 Salisbury Rd, Tsim Sha Tsui
3891 8888
Mon–Sun 12pm–2pm, 6–10.30pm
[MAP p. 173 E3]

Rosewood Hong Kong is a flash and new hotel with a design profile and aesthetic that is second to none. If you can tear yourself away from Indian artist Bharti Kerr's life-size elephant in the lobby and the **Butterfly Patisserie** with the Damian Hirst artwork, you might make it to The Legacy House on the fifth floor. Unlike in other hotels, this Chinese restaurant has a casual-cool vibe without the over the top fine-dining etiquette, and the food quality is top-notch. You can indulge in dim sum and Peking duck, but foodies should be guided by chef Chi Wai Li's inspired seafood cuisine from rural Shunde province in Southern China (where the Cheng family hotel owners hail from originally). Try stir-fried noodles made from rolled fish and delicate wok-fried egg topped with crabmeat and bird's nest. The Wu Tou – a taro, craft vodka, lychee and pandan cocktail – is another adventurous surprise. When not ogling the harbour views, note the portraits by Melbourne street artist Rone.

POCKET TIP

Also at Rosewood, the DarkSide bar features jazz bands, seriously aged whiskey, a chocolate sommelier and a cigar bar. Next door, new K11 Musea, a world-class art and culture-led retail destination, opened in late 2019.

101

8 MOON LOK CHINE/E RE/TAURANT

Unit 2–4, 1st floor, Xiqu
Centre, 88 Austin Road West,
Tsim Sha Tsui
3622 1449
Mon–Sun 9am–11pm
[MAP p. 174 A4]

Arrive here with an appetite,
as Moon Lok focuses on
best-loved dishes from across
China's many provinces.
Located in the new Xiqu
Centre (see p. 96), it's a 200-
seat restaurant that packs
out with families combining
a cultural outing with a
feast. There are big tables
for lazy-Susan-style lunches,
but travellers can bags the
smaller tables with jade green
comfortable back bench seats
or little tables for two. Try the
roasted pork belly and Peking
duck (which needs to be
pre-ordered) that can be seen
hanging in the open kitchen.
Other specialities include the
photogenic baked crab meat
served in its shell, baked snowy
mountain barbeque pork buns,
pan-fried shredded radish cake
and baby oyster omelettes.

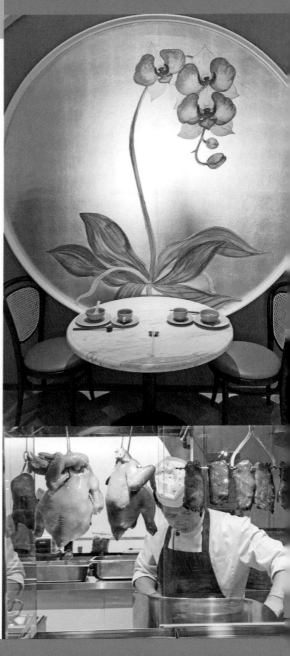

9 OZONE

Level 118, The Ritz-Carlton,
ICC, 1 Austin Rd, West Kowloon
2263 2270
Mon–Thurs 5pm–1am,
Fri 5pm–2am, Sat 3pm–2am,
Sun 12pm–12am
[MAP p. 171 C2]

There is no better place to get high, quite literally. Ozone occupies the very top floor of the ICC's (see p. 99) Ritz-Carlton hotel at a lofty 484 metres (1587 feet). By rights, it can be called the highest bar in the world, which equates to absolutely spectacular views. The interior is ultra-contemporary, with severe angular lines, a marble bar, abstract neon lighting and metallic cubist furniture. Despite its lofty highs, this place attracts a mixed crowd, including office workers and tourists, and it doesn't take itself too seriously. Nab a couch for a laid-back night of cocktails and Japanese tapas. The tempura prawn and avocado maki go down well with a vodka Dragon's Back (with raspberry, elderflower, lime and basil yuzu foam).

10 DADA BAR + LOUNGE

Level 2, The Luxe Manor hotel,
39 Kimberley Rd, Tsim Sha Tsui
3763 8778
Sun–Thurs 2.30pm–1am,
Fri–Sat 2.30pm–2am
[MAP p.174 C4]

Expect the unexpected at this dark cavernous dreamlike space. Inspired by the 20th-century Dadaist movement, which favoured irrationality over reason, this bar – part of the equally surreal boutique The Luxe Manor hotel – is an extravagance, the mood of which is wonderfully complemented by stiff drinks. Heart-shaped chairs sprout golden wings, chandelier 'branches' fall from the ceiling, paisley swirls cover the carpet and red-velvet drapes and studded leather panels line the walls. There's live music from Monday to Saturday, be it jazz or acoustic pop, affordable wines by the glass and a daily happy hour(s) from 4pm until 9pm. Bar snacks include deep-fried calamari, cheese platters and classic nachos. Book ahead (www.dadalounge.com.hk) to guarantee yourself a table.

JORDAN & BEYOND

Beyond harbourside Tsim Sha Tsui in Kowloon lie the urban enclaves of Jordan, Yau Ma Tei, Mong Kok and Prince Edward, in that order. These heavily populated, traffic-dense neighbourhoods are attractions in their own right, given how different they are from relatively orderly Hong Kong Island and even Tsim Sha Tsui and West Kowloon. To make the point, Mong Kok is often cited as being one of the most densely populated places on the planet, and certainly the most populated area in Hong Kong. For the urban traveller, this crammed hip-and-shoulder living is what gives the place its buzz – it's exciting and chaotic.

The suburbs extend along the big retail thoroughfare of Nathan Road, making it easy to navigate off this beaten path into back streets and be fairly confident of making your way back. But be warned: it is a long road and public transport is probably the better option. Access points are at eponymous MTR stops: Jordan, Yau Ma Tei, Mong Kok and Prince Edward on the Tsuen Wan line. (Keep going one stop and you'll hit Sham Shui Po (see p. 118).

Over and above the lively and lived-in atmosphere, outdoor markets are the big crowd-pullers. Head to Jordan for the Jade Market (see p. 110), Yau Ma Tei for Shanghai Street (see p. 109) and Temple Street Night Market (see p. 114), and Prince Edward and Mong Kok for goldfish, flowers and the Ladies' Market (see p. 111).

→ Markets are a highlight of this part of the city

SIGHTS
1. Broadway Cinematheque & Kubrick

SIGHTS & SHOPPING
2. Shanghai Street
3. Jade Market
4. Kowloon Street Markets

SHOPPING
5. Yue Hwa

SHOPPING & EATING
6. Langham Place & Cordis Hotel
7. Temple Street Night Market

EATING
8. Mido Cafe
9. Mak Man Kee Noodle Shop

1 BROADWAY CINEMATHEQUE & KUBRICK

Prosperous Garden, 3 Public
Square St, Yau Ma Tei
2384 8929
Mon–Sun 11.30am–10pm
[MAP p. 174 B2]

Broadway Cinematheque is as
close as it gets to an alternative
and art house cinema in Hong
Kong. With four screens and
a total of 460 seats, it has
a decent line-up of quality
mainstream and arthouse
flicks, classic films, animations
and film-festival favourites.
Fittingly, this cultural hub,
located unassumingly in
the middle of public estate
housing, is also home to
fabulous Kubrick, a cafe and
bookshop where arty types,
cinephiles and students sip
matcha, frappé coffee and iced
tea and sup on pastries and
toasted sandwiches. The space
is huge with a cultured vibe
informed by piles of Chinese
books devoted to (mostly
Western) films, including
biographies of directors
such as Coppola, Tarantino,
Hitchcock and Bergman.
There are occasional pop-up
stalls and a comprehensive
DVD selection of classic films.
Get in local mode with a copy
of In the Mood for Love, a
stunning movie directed by
Wong Kar-wai.

POCKET TIP
Nearby, sweet little Mum
Veggie (Shop 8, Eaton
Hotel, 380 Nathan Rd)
is a Japanese vegetarian
cafe selling simple but
wholesome salads,
organic bread, soups
and the like.

2 SHANGHAI STREET

Yau Ma Tei
Open Mon–Sun 10am–late
[MAP p. 174 B1]

Running parallel to Nathan Road and Temple Street through Jordan, Yau Ma Tei and Mong Kok, Shanghai Street has oodles of history, including a row of old tong lau (tenement) shophouses (at numbers 600–626, towards the Mong Kok end). The Yau Ma Tei section is the most popular, being the destination for retail shops that sell practical kitchenware at wholesale prices. For visitors it's an Aladdin's cave of useful souvenirs. Trawl both sides of the street for shops jam-packed with oversized bamboo dim sum steaming baskets, hand-carved wooden mooncake moulds, thick wooden chopping boards and lethal-looking choppers, which can be sharpened on the spot (but might not make it through customs). The lightweight aluminum beer mugs make the perfect addition to any picnic basket – all you need is the Tsingtao.

POCKET TIP

The 1930s Yau Ma Tei Theatre (6 Waterloo Rd) is a renovated cultural venue where non-Cantonese speakers can immerse in Cantonese opera with the help of English subtitles.

109

3 JADE MARKET

Kansu Street, Yau Ma Tei
Open Mon–Sun 11am–5.45pm
[MAP p. 174 B2]

In 1984, Kowloon's jade hawkers were cleared off the street and relocated to a characterless lot under the flyover at the junction of Kansu and Battery streets. With the addition of a corrugate roof, the trade forged on, and this big shed still attracts a crowd today. The location might not shine but the market atmosphere makes up for it. Inside, hundreds of stallholders clamour together to sell inexpensive jade rings, pendants, amulets and bracelets, along with single pearls, earrings and necklaces. There's a rainbow of semi-precious beads and colourful gem stones plus small figurines and ornaments, including Chinese Zodiac animal pendants, which, for a couple of dollars, make great mementos. Sandra at stall 447 comes highly recommended for semi-precious stones, and Irene at stall 278 is it-and-a-bit for pearls – you buy 'em, she'll string 'em. Take note that high-quality jade is expensive and best bought in a jewellery store or with an expert. Don't forget to haggle – with good humour – it's expected and part of the fun.

POCKET TIP

Tin Hau Temple Complex at 56–8 Temple Street has three heritage temples, a peaceful 'rest garden' and dragon dances on festive occasions.

4 KOWLOON STREET MARKETS

Mong Kok and Prince Edward
All markets open daily
[MAP p. 175 B3]

To Mong Kok, to Mong Kok,
to buy a fat pig … lively and
local Mong Kok is the place
for street shopping with five
popular markets all located
within easy walking distance
of the Mong Kok and Prince
Edward MTR stations. For
bargain buys, head to the
Ladies' Market (Tung Choi
St, Mong Kok, open 11am–
11.30pm) for hair accessories
and beauty products and **Fa
Yuen Street Market** (Mong
Kok and Prince Edward, open
2–11pm) for bargain clothing
and sneakers/runners. If you're
more about sightseeing, head
to the **Goldfish Market**
(43–49 Bute Street, Prince
Edward, open 11am–9.45pm)
to see an excessive number
of plastic bags filled with
brightly coloured aquarium fish
or the **Yuen Po Street Bird
Garden** (37 Flower Market
Rd, open 7am–8pm), which is
amarket designed in the style
of a traditional Chinese garden
and has stalls selling ornate
bamboo cages and chirping
songbirds. If captive animals
unsettle you, then the sweet-
smelling **Flower Market**
(Flower Market Rd, Prince
Edward, open 9.30am–7.30pm)
has auspicious blooms.

POCKET TIP

Sneaker Street, between
Argyle and Soy
intersections on Fa Yuen
Street, is the place to
buy discounted sneaker
brands, including Nike,
Converse and Adidas.

111

5 YUE HWA

301–309 Nathan Rd, Jordan
3511 2222
Mon–Sun 10am–10pm
[MAP p. 174 B3]

Promised people presents? Yue Hwa is like a Chinese version of Australia's Myer or Britain's Marks & Spencer department stores – but with Chinese chintz. This multi-storey department store is the place for picking up well-priced gifts and for finding Chinese products without being bamboozled by bargaining and product authenticity. The ground floor has traditional silk dresses, shirts and dressing gowns, and a selection of Chinese medicine, including shark fin, dried abalone and bird's nests (although avoid these trades, not least because it's doubtful you'd get such items through customs). Upstairs, the range includes jade and amber bangles, Buddha statues, ornamental sculptures, carved wooden screens, antique pots, kitchen ceramics, tea sets, fans and chopsticks. Pyjamas and silk quilts are found here, too. Oh, and mahjong sets and antique snuff bottles and … the list goes on.

6 LANGHAM PLACE & CORDI/ HOTEL

555 Shanghai St, Mong Kok
3552 3028
Langham Place Mon–Sun
11am–11pm
[MAP p. 175 A4]

Sparklingly modern Langham Place stands out amid Mong Kok's older-style architecture. The 15-storey mall has a futuristic central escalator delivering shoppers to global stores and outlets selling mid-range sportswear, lingerie, handbags, shoes, beauty products and electronics. Accessible via a glass walkway, the adjoining Cordis Hotel has an extensive collection of Chinese art, including works by Jiang Shuo and Yue Minjun, and a reputation for excellent guest service. **Ming Court** (open Mon–Sun 11am–3pm and 6–10.30pm) is its lauded Cantonese restaurant with specialties such as coral trout fillet with Chinese black mushroom and dried shrimp roe. **The Garage Bar** (open Mon–Sun from 5pm) is the hotel's tres cool casual courtyard venue. It has two gorgeous vintage Citroën van food trucks serving craft beers (40 kinds, including its home-brewed TGB Golden Ale) and bar bites featuring Impossible Cheeseburgers (vegan), spicy chicken drumlets and French fries.

7 TEMPLE STREET NIGHT MARKET

Temple Street, Yau Ma Tai
Mon–Sun 6–10pm
[MAP p. 174 B3]

Dai pai dongs, or street food markets, used to be popular at the end of a working day but few remain today. Mercifully, this famed example has stood the test of time. Stretching from Man Ming Lane South to Nanking Street (with a temple in the middle), this stretch of outdoor eateries takes over the neighbourhood at sundown. Order take-away oyster pancakes and wontons or sit down at formica tables for a casual banquet of whole steamed fish, clams sautéed in garlic and fried rice. Tsingtao longneck beers are the beverage of choice and there's nothing quite like a chilled one straight from the fridge on a hot humid night. After dinner, stroll around the canvas-topped stalls, selling everything from souvenirs, cheap handbags and clothing to gadgets and electronics.

POCKET TIP

Hongkongfoodietours.com explores the streets eats in Mong Kok, Yau Ma Tei and Jordan on its three-hour Temple Street Night Foodie Tour. The $770 price tag includes tastings at six food stops.

8 MIDO CAFE

Public Square, 63 Temple St,
Yau Ma Tei
2384 6402
Thurs–Tues 9am–9.45pm
[MAP p. 174 B2]

Mido is what Hong Kong cafes used to look like … it's a famous old hangout lauded for its old-school cha chaan teng (local tea-house-style) of eating. What's more, it's in the original 1950s building and not much has changed since it opened. It's located on Public Square with telltale Art Deco-influenced curved walls. Inside, it's all authentic vintage mosaic floor and wall tiles, ceiling fans, wooden booths, and American diner-style vinyl and chrome chairs. The laminated spill-friendly menu is in English and Cantonese and categories include 'soup', 'sandwich & toast', 'spaghetti/macaroni', 'rice' and 'curry/satays'. Cha chaan teng dishes arose from the post-World War II fusion of Cantonese and Western influences. Keep this in mind when ordering Mido's cuisine. Try the signature baked spare rib with tomato sauce and a fried egg and steamed rice, or the nostalgic curried chicken and prawn. For breakfast go true Hong Kong: order the condensed milk and butter toast, and a milk tea.

POCKET TIP

If you're looking for a more contemporary caffeine fix, Cafe REVOL (4–16 Tak Shing St) is an independent cafe with barista coffee and stools overlooking the street.

9 MAK MAN KEE NOODLE /HOP

51 Parkes St, Jordan
2736 5561
Mon–Sun 12pm–12.30am
[MAP p. 174 B3]

It's essential to know the closest good wonton noodle shop no matter which corner of Hong Kong you find yourself in. Mak Man Kee is a traditional Guangdong-style noodle joint that is spot-on for local ambience. The narrow tiled space is lit by fluro lighting and crowded with booths, and its teeny steamy kitchen is tucked behind glass so you can ogle Chinese greens and fresh noodles being prepped as you walk in. It's all very Hong Kong retro. Order the wonton noodle soup, the soup of which is made with dried shrimps and pork bones. The noodles should be springy and al dente. Mak's are freshly made from flour and duck eggs; and the recipe hasn't changed in more than sixty years. Another telltale thumbs-up is the crunch when you bite into the prawn wonton and the delicately thin wrappers. The portions are small, so top up with a side of greens and oyster sauce. Try out some mangled Cantonese greetings and you'll get smiles from the staff.

ʃHAM ʃHUI PO

The zeitgeist in Hong Kong is such that exciting up-and-coming suburbs tend be those on the city fringes where expensive rents have forced small indie and boutique operators into more residential areas. Sham Shui Po defies this trend. While it has hit fandom status in the past five or so years, it's not because it has been gentrified – rather it's the opposite. This working-class Kowloon neighbourhood, north of Prince Edward (*see* the Jordan and Beyond chapter, p. 106) is thought to be the 'real' Hong Kong, with old-school trades and a humble day-to-day character apparent in the street markets, old tofu shops and dried seafood stores. This alone draws a crowd. But Sham Shui Po also attracts ring-ins from other parts of Hong Kong. Artisans and creatives visit to tap into the fabulous wholesale Bead, Button, Leather and Ribbon streets (*see* p. 122), and foodies can't go past countless eateries to sample noodles, dumplings and pineapple buns made from recipes handed down for generations. One of them, Hop Yik Tai (*see* p. 124) has earned itself a Michelin star for its efforts. For travellers, this combination lends itself to an unbeatable immersion.

Sham Shui Po is accessible via the eponymous MTR stop on the Tsuen Wan line. Everything is within easy walking distance from the station.

↤ *Traditional shops and retail brings people to Sham Shui Po*

SIGHTS
1. Market Streets

SHOPPING
2. Bead, Button, Leather & Ribbon Streets
3. Vinyl Hero

EATING
4. Hop Yick Tai
5. Kowloon Restaurant
6. Tim Ho Wan
7. A1 Tofu Company

1 MARKET STREETS

Pei Ho, Ki Lung & Apliu sts
Mon–Sun various opening times
10am–8pm
[MAP p. 176 C2]

For an authentic slice of Hong Kong life, there's hardly a better immersion than a stroll around the shops and market stalls of this proud working-class precinct. It's unlikely you'll buy here, but rather marvel at local life. **Pei Ho Street** has fresh produce stalls characterised by red plastic lamps that light up bunches of Chinese greens and pyramids of shiny apples and pomelos. Rough cuts of pork hang from big steel hooks in the butcher shops and, in the fishmongers, whole fish, their hearts still beating, make for intriguing (if a little uncomfortable) viewing. On **Ki Lung Street** there's a clutch of savoury-smelling dried seafood shops, where inflated fish bladders hang from the ceilings and jars of dried mushrooms, herbs and sea creatures line the wall. **Apliu Street** is a typical market street with a tech-geek theme. You'll see stalls stocked and stacked high with cheap mobile phone accessories, electronics and techy gadgets.

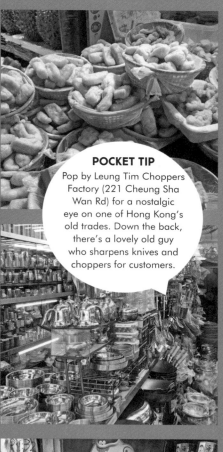

POCKET TIP

Pop by Leung Tim Choppers Factory (221 Cheung Sha Wan Rd) for a nostalgic eye on one of Hong Kong's old trades. Down the back, there's a lovely old guy who sharpens knives and choppers for customers.

2 BEAD, BUTTON, LEATHER & RIBBON STREETS

Yen Chow, Ki Lung, Nam Cheong, Tai Nan & Yu Chau Sts
Mon–Sun 10.30am–8pm
[MAP p. 177 D3]

In the '50s and '60s Sham Shui Po was home to factories that produced textiles and leather. When the factories moved across the border to cheaper digs in mainland China, it was left to locals to make a living from shops selling surplus items from the textiles trade. Now the area has unwittingly found a niche as a hot spot for millennial DIY tailors and crafty types looking for budget buttons, beads and the like in a hedonistic range of colours, sizes and designs. Typically, you'll head to different streets depending on what you're after, be it bolts of fabric (**Yen Chow St Hawker Bazaar** and **Ki Lung St**), colourful ribbons (**Nam Cheong St**), leather (**Tai Nan St**), buttons (**Ki Lung St**) or beads (**Yu Chau St**). Expect to find other eclectic sewing supplies as you stroll around, from tassels, cords and lace to patches, zippers and clasps.

POCKET TIP
Sham Shui Po-made Doughnut backpack shop (68 Fuk Wa St) is a sign that the area is opening up to a new era of contemporary designers.

3 VINYL HERO

Flat D, 5th floor, Wai Hong
Bldg, 239 Cheung Sha Wan Rd
9841 7136
Call before visiting
[MAP p. 176 C1]

Some of the best shops in
Sham Shui Po, and indeed
Hong Kong, are found in
towering apartment blocks
where lower rents make
business sense for small-time
entrepreneurs. One of them
is Vinyl Hero, a music tragic's
heaven, which is squirreled
away on the fifth floor of a
residential building. There is
no fuss or fanfare; the place
is jam-packed warehouse-style
with boxes of – at last count
300,000 – vintage vinyl records.
Owner and collector Paul Au,
a refugee from Vietnam, has
been living here for more than
30 years and has essentially
created a time capsule of
music, favouring genres
from the '60s, '70s and '80s.
Reggae? Funk? Soul? Name
your poison and Au will deftly
relieve the vinyl of its plastic
sleeve and get it spinning.
While it might feel slightly
intimidating shopping in
someone's home, rest assured
it's not unusual in Hong Kong.
Ring ahead to be sure Au is
home before visiting.

4 HOP YICK TAI

121 Kweilin St
2720 0239
Mon–Sun 6.30am–8.30pm
[MAP p. 176 C2]

It's a bit tricky finding Hop Yik Tai, especially if you haven't got around to mastering Cantonese. Keep an eye out for signage and a fit-out that's newer than most on the street – this place is more than 50 years old, but it got an upgrade after winning a Michelin star. Also note the Cantonese ladies serving a queue of hungry punters from a bench outside and a gaggle of standing patrons holding paper plates under their chins. Inside, the tiny eatery has only seven tables, so prepare to go elbow-to-elbow with diners chowing down on plates of heavenly cheong fan – a slippery dish of folded rice noodle rolls topped with soy and hoi sin (plum) sauce, chilli and a scattering of sesame seeds. It's traditionally a breakfast dish, so too the congee that's listed on the wall menu in Cantonese. Try the beef, pork with thousand-year-egg or fish balls. It's comfort food for the soul. And despite the Michelin nod, it's cheap. At a busy Chinese restaurant like this one, it's entirely excusable to stand next to the table of people who look like they're about to leave.

5 KOWLOON RESTAURANT

282 Yu Chau St
3188 9566
Mon–Sun 6.30am–11pm
[MAP p. 176 B1]

Hong Kong's pineapple bun might look like a ho-hum bit of brioche with a crumbly top, but don't be fooled. This humble breakfast bun is a local icon. Kowloon Restaurant, a chan chaan teng (tea house serving Hong Kong cuisine with Cantonese and Western influences) serves authentic burger-sized pineapple buns (called 'jumbo rocky buns' here) in an easygoing dining room with a television and padded booth seats. The buns are made on-the-spot (you can watch them going into the oven) from sugar, eggs, flour and lard, and are fluffy with a crispy top that crumbles on first bite. Note the absence of pineapple – the buns are so-called because the sugar crust has the debatable appearance of pineapple. In any case, they're delicious and should be eaten accompanied by milk tea or stocking tea – a condensed milk and tea concoction. Duck your head into the kitchen to see it being poured from a height through a tea bag that looks like a long stocking.

POCKET TIP

Nearby, Lung Hing Tong (92–4 Ki Lung St) is a stand-out green-tiled building with a dragon on top. Totally Instagrammable.

6 TIM HO WAN

9–11 Fuk Wing St
2788 1226
Mon–Fri 10am–9.30pm,
Sat–Sun 9am–9.30pm
[MAP p. 177 F2]

When the original Tim Ho Wan in Mong Kok earned a Michelin star in 2005, its baked barbeque pork buns became the cheapest Michelin-starred dish in the world. The eatery, which attracted queues that looped around the block, prompted offshoots around the globe that continue to offer top quality, cheap dumplings. This Sham Shui Po incarnation doesn't let the side down. The casual eatery is kitted out to withstand big crowds, with long tables that you can expect to share during rush hour and private booths you might snare during quieter times. The service is no-fuss, with menus as placemats and melamine cups and bowls. Use the slip of pink paper to tick off what you'd like. Order shrimp dumplings and rice rolls with barbeque pork or get adventurous with delicious pan-fried turnip cakes and beef balls with bean curd. Don't go past those sweet-savoury pork buns. You'll wish you ordered more.

POCKET TIP
For delicious handmade dumplings (which you can watch being made in-situ) and wonton soup, also try Yuen Fong Dumplings (104 Fuk Wa St).

7 A1 TOFU COMPANY

103 Kweilin St
Mon–Sun 10.30am–12.30am
[MAP p. 176 B2]

If there is such a thing as a tofu champion, this joint should own the title, with its silky smooth sweet snacks served in little bowls from a streetside counter. The fit-out is typically humble, but the place is actually owned by three young guys tapping into the renewed interest in authentic local food and organic ingredients. The chief ingredient in tofu is soy bean, and A1 makes its tofu from organic Canadian soy beans in gleaming stainless steel machinery at the back of the shop. The cheap ($9-12), high-protein snack is eaten by locals anytime of day. The most traditional tofu is plain but the ginger is pretty good, too. Handy photos on the front of the counter mean you can point to the tofu of choice, sprinkle a tablespoon of ginger and sugar on top and tuck-in standing at the little side bench.

POCKET TIP

Got a sweet tooth? San Lung Cake Shop (68 Pei Ho St) sells traditional Chinese cakes and pastries including delicious black sesame cakes.

127

MACAU

Much is said about Macau's gambling dens, the most elaborate of which, the Venetian, is bigger than its Las Vegas counterpart. But the real drawcard to this former Portuguese colony and China's only other Special Administrative Region is its seamless blend of Portuguese and Cantonese influences. An overnight trip here can reveal a tantalising combination of East meets West, be it in the architecture of the Ruins of St Paul's, and Rua Da Felicidade (*see* p. 130); the Portuguese cuisine at António (*see* p. 135) and Restaurante Fernando (*see* p. 137); or the people and their unique culture.

Sixty kilometres (37 miles) south-west of Hong Kong, Macau consists of a peninsula that narrowly borders China's Guangdong province and the islands of Taipa and Coloane, which have been connected by a section of casino-studded landfill known as the Cotai strip.

Two ferry companies (*see* p. 151) service the one-hour route between Hong Kong's Macau Ferry Terminal on Connaught Road, Central and Macau Taipa Ferry Terminal. Ferries depart every 15 minutes from 7am to 12am, and you'll need your passport. In 2018, the new 55-kilometre-long (34 miles) Hong Kong–Zhuhai–Macau Bridge (*see* p. 151) opened, connecting Hong Kong to Macau (and Zhuhai) by road for the first time. It's a cheaper alternative and more regulare than the ferry service for passengers transiting to Macau from Hong Kong airport, but the ferries are generally still quicker.

→ *The city's casinos stand next to Portuguese architecture*

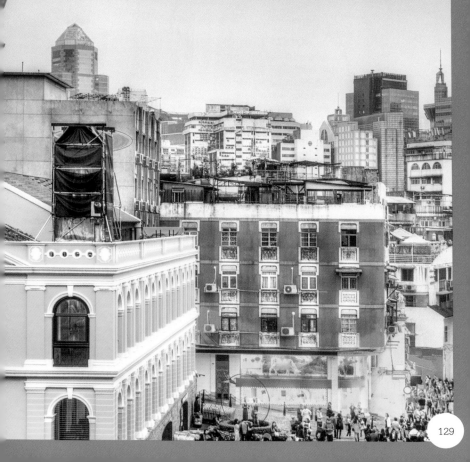

POCKET TIP

Take a 10-minute cab ride to Long Wa Teahouse (3R, Norte Do Me Alm Lacerda), one of three remaining traditional dim sum restaurants, a la 1960s Macau.

RUA DA FELICIDADE

Macau City Centre

For whatever reason, this little street – one of old Macau's most emblematic – has not made the World Heritage register. It will in time, no doubt. A couple of blocks off Avenida de Almeida Ribeiro and a five-minute walk from famous Senado Square, Rua da Felicidade is a thin strip of two-storey, tile-roofed tong lau (tenement buildings) with red shutters, doors and awnings. It was once a hangout for prostitutes, opium dealers, drinkers and gamblers, and thus the name translates to 'Happiness Street'. The rejuvenated version is a serene place to amble past fish tanks, noodle restaurants, bubble teashops and bakeries where the comforting smell of fresh-baked almond cookies fills the air.

MERCEARIA PORTUGUESA

8 Calçada da Igreja de São
Lázaro, Macau City Centre
(853) 2856 2708
Mon–Fri 1–9pm, Sat–Sun
12pm–9pm

In the middle of the
St Lazarus neighbourhood
is **Albergue da Santa
Casa da Misericórdia**, an
enchanting Portuguese square,
shaded by a camphor tree
and bordered by a handful
of businesses, including
Albergue 1601 (*see* p. 132)
and Mercearia Portuguesa
(aka the Portuguese Corner
Shop). A visit to this shop
should induce some serious
mother-country nostalgia. On
old timber shelves you'll find
spicy Portuguese sardines,
bottles of olive oil, pickled
green tomatoes, decadently
wrapped chocolates and old-
fashioned bonbons. Goods
with a Macau touch include
Portuguese tiles, retro soaps
and handmade toys.

POCKET TIP

Macau's St Lazarus
neighbourhood could well
be called Little Lisbon, such
is the character and beauty
of its 16th-century cobbled
streets and shuttered
low-rise houses.

ALBERGUE 1601

8 Calçada da Igreja de São Lázaro, Macau City Centre
(853) 2836 1601
Tues–Thurs & Sun 12pm–11pm, Fri–Sat 12pm–11.30pm

Pull up an alfresco pew at Albergue 1601 and behold the European scenery: a mosaic cobbled square with centuries-old camphor trees surrounded by two-storey Portuguese terraces with buttery yellow walls and wooden shutters (Mercearia Portuguesa (see p. 131) is also here). This beautiful setting makes dining at Albergue hard to resist. The restaurant taps into the zeitgeist of Macau's Portuguese history, with Portuguese-skewed Mediterranean food. Linger at lunch over cheese platters, marinated olives, clams, sardines and white wine. In the evenings, indoor tables are spread throughout the building and laid with white linen and shimmering glassware. It's very romantic. Pair baked duck and rice, grilled octopus or roast suckling pig with European wines from the bottles lining one wall.

POCKET TIP

Meander to one of Macau's best-known landmarks, the Ruins of St Paul's, a 17th-century church facade that, despite its decrepit state, sits nobly and quite spectacularly on a hilltop in the old town.

POCKET TIP
Riquexo is an authentic Macanese restaurant tucked away in a quiet nearby neighbourhood (69 Avenida Sidonio Pais). The owner – Aida de Jesus – is over 100 years old and speaks the language of Patua, a disappearing dialect.

POCKET TIP

Rua do Cunha itself has little shops and stalls selling local street treats. Try the pork pastries at Fong Kei (14 Rua do Cunha) and durian ice-cream at Mok Yee Kei (9 Rua do Cunha).

CUNHA BAZAAR

33–35 Rua do Cunha, Old Taipa Village
(853) 2882 7989
Mon–Sun 9.30am–10pm

Painted bright yellow and covered in murals, two-storey Cunha Bazaar has become a landmark in Old Taipa Village (*see* p. 135), specialising in made-in-Macau merchandise. Downstairs, polished-concrete floors and nostalgic wallpaper provide the setting for Macau's offbeat culinary treats – spicy dried fish, shrimp-flavoured peanuts and coconut egg rolls with shredded pork jerky, all packaged to take home. Upstairs a slightly kitsch space is dedicated to Macau's iconic *Soda Panda* TV cartoon characters, with gimmicky T-shirts, postcards and almond cakes in retro boxes. Rua do Cunha's traditional Macau morsels make perfectly packaged gifts that will pass customs inspections. They include almond cookies with pork filling, ginger candy and durian agar-agar pudding.

ANTÓNIO

7 Rua dos Clerigos, Old Taipa
Village
(853) 2888 8668
Mon–Sun 11.30am–4pm &
6–10.30pm

Among the restaurants and
bars of Old Taipa Village
is António, a Portuguese
restaurant with exterior
mosaic tiles and wooden
wine kegs. António Coelho
has won accolades for his
authentic cuisine and excellent
intimate service (he's often
here circulating among the
tables). Starters include
Portuguese octopus salad and
goat's cheese au gratin with
olive oil and honey. For mains,
indulge in suckling pig or lamb
rack with potatoes au gratin.
There's a decent vegetarian
offering, including spiced
couscous cakes with hummus.
Ask for a table downstairs
away from the kitchen.

POCKET TIP

Only minutes away from
the casino area known
as Cotai strip, Old Taipa
Village is an unexpected
local gem with quaint
alleys, renovated Chinese
shophouses and colonial
buildings, all aglow with
street lamps.

POCKET TIP

Take some time to explore the sites of quaint Coloane village, including cobbled Eduardo Marques Square and the waterfront promenade, the Chapel of St Francis Xavier and Old Tin Ha Temple.

LORD /TOW'/ BAKERY

1 Rua do Tassara, Coloane
(853) 2888 2534
Mon–Sun 7am–10pm

In 1989, English expat Andrew Stow created a hybrid recipe between Portuguese pastel de nata and English custard tarts. To differentiate between the familiar local 'egg tart', resident Chinese people dubbed them 'Portuguese egg tarts'. Stow's recipe caught on in Macau and became an edible icon for visitors and locals alike. The company that produces the tarts, Lord Stow's Bakery, has outlets in Hong Kong, Korea, Japan, Taiwan and the Philippines, and sells 10,000-plus pieces on average each day, which is testimony to how tasty they are. This bakery is the original, but there are four other local offshoots, two of which are nearby.

RESTAURANTE FERNANDO

9 Praia de Hac Sa, Coloane
(853) 2888 2264
Mon–Sun 12pm–9.30pm

Hongkongers take daytrips to Macau just to have lunch at Fernando's – it's almost a rite of passage. This is Macau's most famed restaurant, a no-fuss, no-reservations venue that promises a rare breed of casual dining. Locals tend to sit up front in a plain room with yellow bricks and louvre windows, but the rear is better. Out back there's a beer garden and a faux rustic pavilion with ceiling fans, dark-wood beams, high ceilings and chequered tablecloths. Wherever you sit, the Portuguese fare stacks up, be it salty baccalau (cod) or stuffed octopus stew and a jug of Sangria. After feasting, finish with a walk on the fine black sand of **Hac Sa Beach**.

LAMMA ILAND

Hong Kong has an incredible 262 outlying islands, offering fun-filled and exploratory daytrips that promise beaches, walks, local food, fresh air and more. Lamma Island, a half-hour ferry ride from Hong Kong Central to the main village of Yung Shue Wan (see p. 140), is one of the best. While much of Hong Kong keeps growing and developing at a heart-stopping rate, Lamma manages to hold onto its hippie reputation and is a sanctuary from the hustle and bustle. The vibe rubs off on even the shortest stay. Stroll around the little rural plots, check out offbeat shops and eateries and walk across the island on the well-known Family Trail Walk (see p. 141). Indulge in local traditions, such as a dumpling breakfast at Sampan Seafood Restaurant (see p. 140) or enjoy a seafood binge at Rainbow Seafood Restaurant (see p. 142).

At time of writing, the North Lamma Heritage and Cultural showroom (at the public library on the left as you walk into town from the Yung Shue Wan pier) was due to open. It's set to be 'a social and cultural hub where both locals and visitors can mingle and share their appreciation of the unique local culture, history, lifestyle and knowledge'.

The main ferry from Hong Kong Central pulls into the old pier in the characteristic main village of Yung She Wan, a car-less place whose residents get around on bicycles (the rusty likes of which are crowded near the ferry pier) and so-called Vee Vee's (little council four-wheelers with VV numberplates).

⇥ Yueng Shue Wan Temple incense sticks

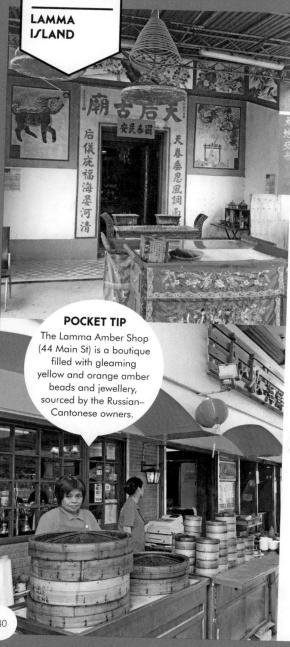

POCKET TIP

The Lamma Amber Shop (44 Main St) is a boutique filled with gleaming yellow and orange amber beads and jewellery, sourced by the Russian–Cantonese owners.

YUNG SHUE WAN VILLAGE

Not much changes in Yung Shue Wan: the Cantonese seafood joints, quirky coffee shops and outdated Western-style bars have been the same for the past decade, but that's all part of the charm. Kick off with a breakfast at **Sampan Seafood Restaurant** – an authentic dim sum eatery with tables right on the water's edge. On the pavement, oversized bamboo steamers filled with pork buns and dumplings usually tempt passers-by. Spend time walking around the little flat-roofed houses, home to yapping dogs and chatty neighbours, and saunter in and out of laneways sporting pot plants of pink bougainvillea. There are a few cafes, but cosy **Bookworm** stands the test of time for a peaceful cup of tea. From here you'll likely get a whiff of the incense burning at **Tin Hau Temple**, which offers a humble little slice of Cantonese life.

FAMILY TRAIL WALK

The Family Trail Walk, beginning in Yung Shue Wan village, is one of Hong Kong's most popular walks, probably because it is nothing too taxing. It is an easy one-hour stroll along a concrete pavement, but it covers pleasant terrain. Lush tropical gardens, little shrines, rural houses, basic eateries and ocean viewpoints along the way mean there is always something to look at. One of the highlights is **Hung Shing Yeh Beach**, a shaded strip of sand where you can hang out and swim (just ignore the three power station stacks looking north). At the other end of the trail, enjoy a seafood lunch at a strip of restaurants in **Sok Kwu Wan village** (*see* p. 142). There's a shuttle boat from here out to **Lamma Fisherfolk's Village**, which floats on a pontoon on the harbour. It's a tourism initiative to help preserve Lamma's seafaring traditions and has some intrigues, including authentic old dragon boats and a tour of a wooden sampan boat, formerly home of a local family. Alternatively, you can head directly back to Hong Kong's Central on the ferry from the village.

POCKET TIP

Keep an eye out for Ah Por Tofu Fa on the right-hand side after you cross Reservoir Road. It's a trailside stall selling nourishing bowls of tofu by day.

SOK KWU WAN SEAFOOD RESTAURANT STREET

First St, Sok Kwu Wan

Sok Kwu Wan is the second biggest of Lamma's villages, a tiny place buoyed by a strip of waterfront seafood restaurants with quality food and a quaint setting that draw day crowds – en masse – from Hong Kong. The eateries have fish tanks bubbling outside and are cheery and colourful, with bright orange tablecloths and plastic chairs in a rainbow of colours. The open sides mean diners can peer onto the boats lined up on the water. The eateries offer similar fare – mostly traditional Cantonese seafood dishes – and tourists tend to judge them by the quality of the fish and crustaceans on the footpath. **Rainbow Seafood Restaurant** (23–7 First St, Sok Kwu Wan) is one of the good ones. This spick-and-span place has a dozen or so round tables making it look like a cheesy wedding venue, which is typical and all part of the fun. They're neatly set with melamine bowls, plates, chopsticks and hand wipes – that kind of thing. The food is magic – spin the lazy Susan for deep fried salt and pepper squid, steamed scallop with garlic sauce and sautéed whole garoupa (local fish) with celery.

LANTAU I/LAND

Hong Kong's largest island is home to Hong Kong International Airport (see p. 150) so chances are you will have seen some of its undulating mountain greenery from the sky. But there's plenty more to explore on the ground, especially if you are in Hong Kong on a longer stay.

The big-name attractions of Po Lin Monastery and Tian Tan Buddha (see p. 147) and Ngong Ping 360 cable car (see p. 146), despite being heavily touristed, are worthwhile outings and offer city alternatives of a nature-based variety. A little further afield, the stilt village of Tai O (see p. 148), is also on the tourist radar, but the remote location and the unique eye on a slower way of life make this a must-do with crowds or without.

Beach lovers are also spoiled for choice, and if you need a fix of white sand and clear water, make a day of it by jumping on a ferry from Central to get to laid-back places such as Lower Cheung Sha Beach (see p. 149).

→ *Lantau Island's Tian Tan Buddha*

POCKET TIP

The Nei Lak Shan Country Trail, stretching across the Ngong Ping Plateau is the well-trodden path you can see from the Ngong Ping 360 cable car.

NGONG PING 360 CABLE CAR

11 Tat Tung Road, Tung Chung
3666 0606
Mon–Fri 10am–6pm, Sat–Sun
9am–6.30pm

Travelling 5.7 kilometres (3.5 miles) over dazzling tropical greenery, this scenic cable car offers a spectacular view of North Lantau Country Park and the South China Sea beyond. The 25-minute journey begins in Tung Chung (from the terminal adjacent to Tung Chung MTR station) and crosses Tung Chung Bay before turning 60 degrees towards North Lantau. From the glass cable cars, you'll have a panorama from which to spot **Hong Kong International Airport** and, threading off into the distance, the new 50-kilometre **Hong Kong–Zhuhai–Macau Bridge** (see p. 151). On a clear day you can see Macau. But most impressive, is eyeing the 34-metre (111.5 feet) bronze-framed **Tian Tan Buddha** (*see* p. 147) as it comes slowly into view over the brow of a hill. There's a culturally themed village at the end of the ride, but most visitors are here for **Po Lin Monastery** (*see* p. 147) and the Tian Tan Buddha. Be mindful that cable car queues at the end of the day are lengthy. Depart early or allow a couple of hours to get back to Tung Chung. Weekdays are quieter.

PO LIN MONA/TERY &
TIAN TAN BUDDHA

Ngong Ping
2985 5248
Mon–Sat 8am–6pm
Cafe Mon–Fri 11.30am–
4.30pm, Sat–Sun 11.30am–7pm

A short walk from Ngong Ping 360 cable car terminal (*see* p. 146), Po Lin Monastery is a Buddhist temple complex that seems lost in time, despite the number of tourists strolling around its marigold pot plants and impressive tiled-roof architecture. The **Main Shrine Hall of Buddha** is the most majestic – the seven span structure is inspired by palatial architectural designs of the Ming and Qing dynasties, but even the small temples are resplendent with their red-lipped double gabled rooftops, colourful flowers, incense and offerings. Simple and affordable vegetarian lunch dishes are available from the **cafe** before a stroll to the Tian Tan Buddha. It might look ancient, but this giant Buddha was built in 1993. The 34-metre (111.5 feet) bronze statue sits poised and untroubled on a hilltop a few metres from the monastery. Master the 268 steps to the top for a fine view of the surrounding country park.

POCKET TIP

Hong Kong Disneyland is on Lantau's Penny Bay at Disneyland Resort (where you can stay in fairytale hotel accommodation). It's the smallest Disneyland, but the Adventureland section is the biggest.

POCKET TIP

Don't be fooled by tour operators promoting pink dolphin tours. It remains to be seen whether the development of the Hong Kong–Zhuhai–Macau bridge devastated their already fragile natural habitat.

TAI O

A short bus ride away from Po Lin Monastery and Tian Tan Buddha (*see* p. 147) and the terminal of Ngong Ping 360 cable car (*see* p. 146) is the fascinating and extremely endearing stilt fishing village of Tai O. By Hong Kong standards, this place, located at the mouth of the Pearl River Delta on the southern-most point of the country, is remote, but it's worth the journey for a peep at traditional life. Once a thriving fishing village, Tai O fell victim to over-fishing, and by the '70s much of the population had left for the big smoke. Those that stayed have (wittingly or otherwise) helped maintain the architectural heritage, traditions and old fisherfolk ways. Take a boat ride to see the stilt houses from the water, wander around the streets and visit shops selling dried fish and jars of salty fish paste. Not to be missed (and the only accommodation option) is luxury **Tai O Heritage Hotel** (www.taioheritagehotel.com) in the former marine police station. The renovation is the work of Hong Kong Heritage Conservation Foundation Limited, praised for putting local history, culture, people and jobs first. The rooftop cafe is a decent option for Cantonese (fried rice with local shrimp paste) and European dishes (club sandwiches).

BEACHE/

The further from Hong Kong Island, the clearer and cleaner the water becomes. Lantau's southern beaches, facing the South China Sea, tend to have white sand, crystal waters and lazy trees. They're sufficiently off-the-beaten track for an adventure, and it's wise to pre-plan by checking walking trails and ferry and bus timetables before departure. Certainly don't expect the creature comforts, snazzy bars and resort-style facilities typical in places like Repulse Bay. The pristine water on a big arc of blonde sand at Mui Wo's **Silvermine Bay Beach** is the most convenient. It's accessible on a direct Mui O ferry from Central. From here, there's a walking trail (or a 10-minute local bus ride) to **Pui O Beach**, another laid-back scenic spot with a serene temple and a small kiosk that rents surfboards to beginners (the waves lap rather than pound). A little further again (a 20-minute local bus ride) **Lower Cheung Sha Beach** has a breezy all-day restaurant called **Bathers**, with a menu that favours Australian cuisine and produce (prawns, wagyu beef and pavlova). The sea view and cold beer make you feel a long way from everywhere. These beaches can also be accessed via taxi rides from Tung Chung station on the Tung Chung MTR line.

GETTING TO HONG KONG

Hong Kong International Airport, known as Chek Lap Kok (www.hkairport.com), is located 45 kilometres (28 miles) from Central Hong Kong on Lantau Island. It is lauded as one of the world's best airports, with efficient baggage reclaim and typically queue-less immigration terminals. Following are some options for getting to and from Chek Lap Kok.

Airport Express

Almost always the best option, this train whisks passengers from the airport into Hong Kong MTR station (via Tsing Yi and Kowloon stations) every 10 to 12 minutes daily between 5.54am and 12.48am. The entire journey takes 24 minutes (which is much quicker than a taxi) and costs $110 one-way and $205 return. You can also purchase a tourist pass (www.mtr.com.hk), which offers return Airport Express tickets and three days of unlimited MTR travel for $350 (with a $50 refund on return of ticket).

On leaving, Hong Kong and Kowloon MTR stations have free check-in services open 24 to 1.5 hours before departure. It's spectacularly functional and means you can jump onto the Airport Express baggage-free.

Taxi

Taxis are very accessible from the airport and are not overly expensive. Follow the signs to the queue (it's never very long). Red taxis service Hong Kong Island and Kowloon, blue taxis service Lantau Island and green taxis service the New Territories. Fares are metered and getting ripped off is rare. The journey to Central will cost between $300 and $420, including tolls, plus $6 extra for each piece of luggage in the boot. The journey time is about 45 minutes; add an extra 30 minutes if you're hitting the city during peak hour times.

GETTING AROUND HONG KONG

Diverse yet efficient is the catchcry for Hong Kong transport, a combination of underground railway (MTR), light rail, buses, minibuses, ferries, trams and (the world's longest) escalator. It's worth buying an **Octopus card** (www.octopuscards.com) for hassle-free access to all modes of transport. A scanner will automatically deduct payments as you tap onto transport.

MTR

The MTR (www.mtr.com.hk) has nine clean and efficient underground lines (including the East Rail line for travel between Hong Kong and Shenzhen) and an Airport Express link. New lines and extensions include the South Island line to Aberdeen and Wong Chuck Hang. The MTR boasts 'passengers consistently arriving at their destinations on time 99% of the time'.

Buses

Air-conditioned one- and two-deck buses crisscross main streets throughout Hong Kong Island and the New Territories, stopping at well-signed dedicated bus stops. Fares are based on distance. Use an Octopus card (see above) to tap on and off the bus or give correct change.

Minibuses

Minibuses require a bit more local knowledge. They cater to small streets and can be flagged down. Once they're full, minibuses won't stop for a new passenger until a seat becomes available. Green minibuses have specific routes at fixed prices, whereas red minibus routes are not always fixed and passengers can get on and off anywhere along the route. You pay as you alight on red minibuses and the driver can usually provide change for small notes.

Ferries

Star Ferries

Star Ferries (see p. 94, www.starferry.com.hk) service Victoria Harbour with piers at Tsim Sha Tsui, Central and Wan Chai. They run Monday to Friday between 7.30am and 11.30pm, depending on the route, with shortened hours on weekends. The double-decker green vessels act mainly as commuter transport, but a trip is a must-do for tourists. The fares are famously low. Purchase a token at the pier before you board or tap on and off with an Octopus card (*see* p. 150). It's a fabulous way to admire the Hong Kong city skyline.

Outlying Island Services

Ferries operating from the Central ferry piers near IFC Mall on Hong Kong Island provide services to Peng Chau, Cheung Chau, Lamma Island and Lantau Island, including Discovery Bay.

Two types of ferries operate along most routes: standard ferries (fares vary) and the slightly more expensive fast ferries. At least one island outing is a Hong Kong-must.

Macau Ferries

Two ferry companies service the Hong Kong Island–Macau route. Ferries depart from the Macau Ferry Terminal on Connaught Road in Central daily every 15 minutes from 7am to 12am. The trip takes approximately one hour. Tickets cost about $320 one-way and can be bought from self-service ticket kiosks at the terminal. With a valid ticket, you can take an earlier ferry if there are seats available. Don't forget your passport – no, I'm not joking!

Hong Kong–Zhuhai–Macau Bridge

This new 55 kilometre (34 miles) bridge (www.hzmb.gov.hk) – the longest bridge-tunnel system sea-crossing in the world–links Lantau Island in Hong Kong to Zhuhai and Macau. Visitors can take buses connecting the Passenger Clearance Building near Hong Kong Airport on one side and Zhuhai and Macau on the other. Fares for shuttle buses cost $65–70 during regular service, but off-peak times journeys attract half-price discounts. It's a cheaper, more regular alternative for passengers transiting to Macau from Hong Kong Airport and it runs 24 hours.

Hong Kong–Guangzhou train

Hong Kong's $11 billion bullet train (mtr.com.hk/highspeed) to Shenzhen and Guangzhou opened in 2018. The 26 kilometre (16 miles) High Speed Rail section in Hong Kong runs from West Kowloon station and connects Hong Kong with Shenzhen and Guangzhou, along with 58 major Mainland stations with no interchanges. Long-haul destinations include Shanghai, Chongquin, Tianjin and Beijing. It runs at 200km/h (124 mph) in the Hong Kong section and up to 350km/h (217 mph) on the Mainland. The first and last trains depart at around 7am and 11pm daily. Journey times vary.

Peak Tram

Opened in 1988, the old-school Peak Tram (runnning 7am to 12am Monday to Sunday) departs every 10 to 15 minutes from the lower Peak Tram terminus on Garden Road, Central. The seven-minute journey through skyscrapers and rainforest is at an almost impossible angle, making this the steepest funicular railway in the world. It's worthwhile doing once, but beware the queues. At time of writing, the Peak Tram was being overhauled to install 210 new passenger tramcars. It remains to be seen if the heritage experience retains its authenticity.

Mid-levels Escalator

The Mid-Levels Escalator (*see* p. 4) is a free commuter mover that runs between Queens Road Central and Conduit Road in Mid-Levels, bisecting 14 streets in the process. It operates between 6am and 12am Monday to Sunday (downhill 6am to 10am, uphill 10am to 12am). It's an excellent option if you're exploring the steep streets of Soho. The suburb of Sai Ying Pun, between Sheung Wan and Kennedy Town, has also had a similar escalator installed.

Trams

Trams (*see* p.2, www.hktramways.com) traverse east–west across Hong Kong Island on six routes (covering 30 kilometres/18 miles) that run between Shau Kei Wan, Happy Valley and Kennedy Town. At peak hours you'll be lucky to bag a seat, but in down times a front seat on the top deck is a window into the frenetic and varied street life of Hong Kong. Trams run from 5am to 12am Monday to Sunday and cost $2.60 & 1.30 (adult/child) per trip. Pay as you get off with cash or an Oyster card (*see* p. 150).

Walking

You'll do a lot of walking in Hong Kong – it's how you'll stumble across some of your best finds – so wear a good pair of shoes and carry bottled water with you. Be prepared for steep slopes on Hong Kong Island and note that it can be incredibly slippery if it's raining. Avoid jaywalking at major crossings in Central, as fines are readily issued if you're caught.

Taxis

Taxis are easy to flag down and cheap compared with other large cities. An average ride on Hong Kong Island costs approximately $40 to $60.

Taxi Tips

Taxis are usually easily hailed along the street, but taxi queues and taxi stands are common at hotels, train stations and shopping malls.

Taxis are available when the rooftop light is on and a red circular sign in the front window is showing. Rectangular red signs in the front window denote Kowloon taxis. If you catch one of these from Hong Kong Island to Kowloon or vice versa you only pay tunnel tolls for one direction.

If you're on Hong Kong Island and want to go to Kowloon, or vice versa, hail an obliging cab by making a wavy motion with your hand to denote going under the water and through the tunnel. It's local knowledge.

Taxi doors open and close on their own!

Ask your hotel clerk or concierge to tell taxi drivers where you are going.

Take your hotel business card or accommodation address with you when going out and give it to taxi drivers when you want to get back.

PUBLIC HOLIDAYS

Most shops and restaurants remain open during public holidays, though some might close for two days over Chinese New Year. Some traditional shops and restaurants and small family owned restaurants may stay closed for longer at this time. For a full list of public holidays see: www.gov.hk.

FESTIVALS & EVENTS

Chinese New Year
(late January/early February)
Hong Kong Arts Festival
(www.hk.artsfestival.org; February/March)
Taste of Hong Kong
Food festival (hongkong.tastefestivals.com; March)
Art Basel
International art show
(www.artbasel.com/hongkong; March)
Cheung Chau Bun Festival
(April/May/June)
Affordable Art Fair Hong Kong
(affordableartfair.com/hongkong; May)
Dragon Boat Festival
(June)
Hong Kong International Film Festival
(www.hkiff.org.hk; August)
Mid-Autumn Festival
(late September/early October)
Beertopia
craft brew festival
(www.starstreet.com.hk; October/December)
Clockenflap
An awesome offbeat waterfront music festival. (www.clockenflap.com; October/November).

ARTS

There is an arts scene in Hong Kong and there are plenty of festivals, but they can be hard to pin down. Check out the lifestyle sections on Friday, Saturday and Sunday in the **South China Morning Post** (www.scmp.com), the city's major English-language daily broadsheet.

Also see websites:

www.lifestyleasia.com/hk (cuisine and luxury living focus)

www.sassyhongkong.com (what's on guide with a female skew)

www.timeout.com/hong-kong (comprehensive guide to restaurants, gigs, galleries and events)

EATING & DRINKING

Menus at international restaurants in Hong Kong are written in English and many local venues also have an English-version menu under the counter. In this book, we've broken listings down as follows: places listed under an Eating heading generally don't sell alcohol but often serve tea and coffee; those listed under Eating & Drinking serve food, tea, coffee and booze (usually).

Most restaurants, cafes and bars are open seven days a week (if they shut it will usually be on a Monday or Tuesday). They tend to open late, around 11am and close around 10pm. Unless foreign-operated, cafes don't open until midday or later – locals tend to drink their coffee around 3pm.

In the higher-end restaurants and bars it's almost always a good idea to book ahead, especially on Friday and Saturday nights. Some hipper bars and restaurants won't take bookings. These should probably be avoided on weekends unless, of course, you're okay with getting sloshed at the bar while you're waiting for a table.

Smoking is not allowed inside restaurants and bars, but many venues have an alfresco area for this purpose.

Pour other people's drinks – especially tea – as much as possible (especially before pouring your own).

Chopstick etiquette

When using chopsticks, don't stick them upright in a bowl of rice – this is a funeral custom. Also, don't pass food to or take food from other people using your own chopsticks – look for the communal chopsticks next to each dish (they're usually a different colour).

At markets and noodle shops you'll sometimes be given a bowl of hot water to wash your own rice bowls and chopsticks. This is customary, a hangover from less hygienic times. Roll with it by giving your utensils a dip, then the water will be taken away.

HYGIENE

After the SARS epidemic in 2002, Hongkongers became fastidious about hygiene. Public washrooms and hand sanitisers can be found at most tourist sites and in shopping malls. Lift buttons and escalator handrails are all slavishly wiped down regularly.

WATER

Hong Kong tap water conforms to the World Health Organisation's recommended guidelines for drinking-water quality, but it doesn't taste great.

Some restaurants and bars will supply tap water on request. When they don't, it's usually because plumbing systems in the older buildings can render the water undrinkable.

Bottled water is readily available in restaurants, supermarkets and so on. Opt for glass if available.

MANNERS

Manners are important in Hong Kong, so always be as polite as possible, especially to the elderly. 'Face' is everything, so avoid losing your cool at all costs, despite the frustrations a different culture can throw at you.

Take off your shoes before entering a house.

If you're sick with a cold, buy a face mask – they're to protect other people, not you.

While shopping, it is routine for shop assistants to follow you around the store so they're at the ready when you have a question. In some other countries, this might only happen if you're suspected of being a shoplifter. Never fear, they're only being helpful. Best to grin and bear it.

TELEPHONE

Hong Kong's country code is 852. To call outside Hong Kong dial +, then the country code or 001, then the country code. All phone numbers, including mobiles, have eight digits.

GSM-compatible phones can be used in Hong Kong. The network coverage includes tunnels and the MTR.

SIM cards can be purchased at 7-Eleven or Circle K stores relatively cheaply (approximately $100) with minimal administration. Even better, **Discover Hong Kong Tourist SIM Cards** (www. discoverhongkong.com) offer all-inclusive and immediately accessible five-day ($88) and eight-day ($118) packages, including a Macau data-roaming package.

Given almost everyone in Hong Kong has a mobile, public phones are fast becoming redundant, however, phone-card and coin-operated phones can still be found at MTR stations and major shopping hubs.

GPS & MAPS

Smart-phone GPS devices are unreliable in Hong Kong, due to the height and density of the city's buildings. Use an old-fashioned map instead, readily available from hotels and at the end of this guidebook.

WI-FI

Internet access is fast, reliable and often free in Hong Kong. Most hotels and hostels have internet facilities, and many coffee shops, cafes and pubs have free wi-fi, where courtesy dictates you buy a drink or snack. You can connect to the internet with a mobile device near the 'MTR Free Wi-Fi Hotspot' sign at every MTR station. It offers free connectivity for 15 minutes per session, with a maximum of five sessions per smart phone/tablet/device per day.

ELECTRICAL APPLIANCES

The majority of electrical outlets in Hong Kong take a three-pronged UK-style plug.

MONEY

Hong Kong's currency is the Hong Kong dollar. All prices quoted in this book are in HK$. It is pegged to the US dollar at a rate of about HK$7.80 to US$1, although exchange rates fluctuate slightly.

It comes in denominations of notes: HK$1000, HK$500, HK$100, HK$50, HK$20 and HK$10, and in coins: HK$10, HK$5, HK$2, HK$1, HK$0.50, HK$0.20 and HK$0.10.

The currency is used in both Hong Kong and Macau, as the two regions are of close proximity and their currencies have similar exchange rates.

At Hong Kong International Airport, currency exchange counters are open from early morning until late at night and many located within the city stay open into the evening.

Most cash machines (ATMs) take international cards and can be found on streets and outside banks. You'll also find ATMs in 7-Elevens.

Tipping is big in Hong Kong. A 10% tip will be automatically added to your bill, and often people tip another 5% to 10% on top of this. More recent hipster venues are boasting 'no service charges', instead asking customers to judge the service. Unless you have a bad experience, it would be considered pretty tight not to tip.

WEATHER

The best times to visit are from March to May and October to November, when the heat and humidity are manageable and the temperature commonly sits between 20–27 degrees Celsius (62–82 Fahrenheit).

USEFUL PHRASES

Cantonese people rarely expect gweilos (foreigners) to speak their lingo as the nine tones make it a difficult language to master. On Hong Kong Island, most people in hotels and the wider service industry will usually speak some English. Taxi drivers usually speak just enough to get you to your destination. But like anywhere, it's always appreciated when you have a go, so give some of these basic sayings a try.

Hello: lay ho

How are you?: lay gay ho a maa?

Good morning: jo san

Goodbye: baai baai

Thank you: ng goy

The bill please?: my dun?

Stop here: leedo

Keep the change: mmsay ee jow

How much is it?: gay daw chin?

Where is the ... ?: hai bin doe ...?

Airport: gay cheung

Bus stop: baa si jaam

Post office: yau guk

Hotel: jau dim

Subway station: day tit jaam

ATM: ji dung tai fun gay

TOURIST INFORMATION

Tourist Information Centres provide leaflets and online information (available 24 hours). Tours can also be booked at all visitor centres.

The tourism board website (www.discoverhongkong.com) is a great source of easily navigable information.

You will find Tourism Information Centres at these locations:

Hong Kong International Airport (Transfer Area E2, Buffer Halls A and B, Arrivals Level T1; Monday to Sunday 8am to 9pm)

The Peak Piazza (between the tower and galleria; Monday to Sunday 11am to 8pm)

Star Ferry Concourse (Tsim Sha Tsui, Kowloon; Monday to Sunday 8am to 8pm)

West Kowloon station (B2 Level, Arrival Concourse, times vary).

EMERGENCIES

Call 999 for local police, ambulance service, fire department and other emergency services.

UNREST

At time of writing (November 2019), the Australian Department of Foreign Affairs and Trade had issued a warning to travellers to 'exercise a high degree of caution' when in Hong Kong due to ongoing public protests throughout the city. It advises visitors to exercise caution by being alert, avoiding protests and demonstrations and moving to a safe place if there are signs of disorder. For updates, monitor local media and follow: https://smartraveller.gov.au

CONSULATE-GENERALS

Australia:
23/F 25 Harbour Rd, Wan Chai
2827 8881
hongkong.china.embassy.gov.au
Monday to Friday 9am–5pm

Britain:
1 Supreme Court Rd, Admiralty
2901 3000
www.gov.uk/world/organisations/british-consulate-general-hong-kong
Monday to Friday 8.30am–5pm

Canada:
9th Floor, Berkshire House, 25 Westlands Rd, Quarry Bay
3719 4700
www.canadainternational.gc.ca
Monday to Friday 8.30am–5pm

New Zealand:
Room 6501, 18 Harbour Rd, Wan Chai
2525 5044
www.mfat.govt.nz
Monday to Friday 8.30am–1pm & 2–5pm.

United States:
26 Garden Rd, Central
2523 9011
hk.usconsulate.gov
Monday to Friday 8.30am–12.30pm & 1.30–5.30pm

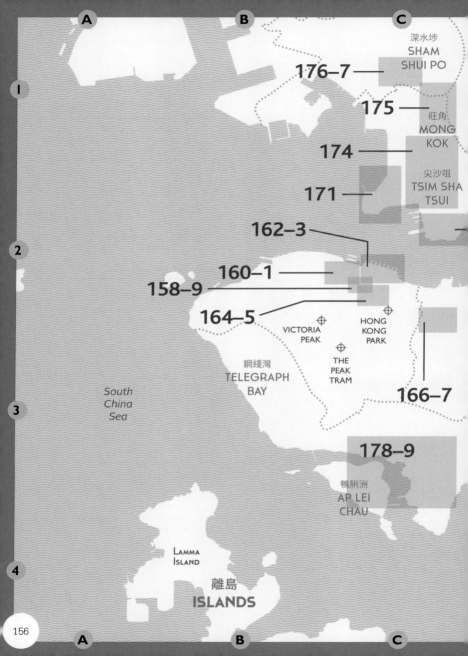

176–7

175

旺角
MONG
KOK

174

尖沙咀
TSIM SHA
TSUI

171

深水埗
SHAM
SHUI PO

162–3

160–1

158–9

164–5

VICTORIA
PEAK

HONG
KONG
PARK

THE
PEAK
TRAM

166–7

鋼綫灣
TELEGRAPH
BAY

South
China
Sea

178–9

鴨脷洲
AP LEI
CHAU

LAMMA
ISLAND

離島
ISLANDS

A   B   C

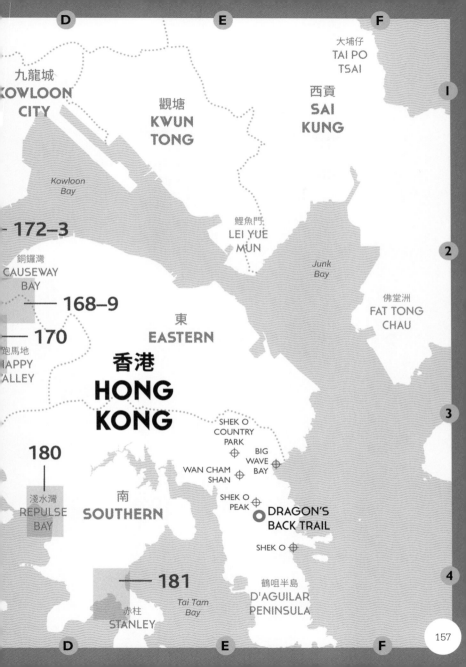

大埔仔
TAI PO
TSAI

九龍城
KOWLOON
CITY

觀塘
KWUN
TONG

西貢
SAI
KUNG

I

Kowloon
Bay

— 172–3

鯉魚門
LEI YUE
MUN

2

銅鑼灣
CAUSEWAY
BAY

Junk
Bay

佛堂洲
FAT TONG
CHAU

— 168–9

東
EASTERN

— 170

跑馬地
HAPPY
VALLEY

香港
HONG
KONG

SHEK O
COUNTRY
PARK

3

180

BIG
WAVE
BAY

WAN CHAM
SHAN

淺水灣
REPULSE
BAY

南
SOUTHERN

SHEK O
PEAK

DRAGON'S
BACK TRAIL

SHEK O

— 181

鶴咀半島
D'AGUILAR
PENINSULA

4

赤柱
STANLEY

Tai Tam
Bay

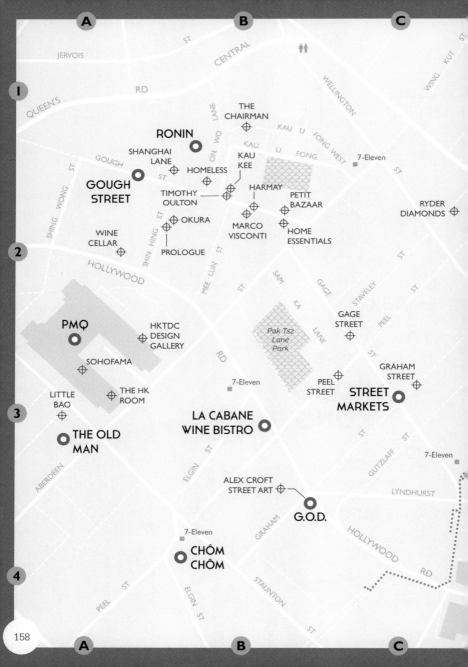

A   B   C

JERVOIS ST

CENTRAL ST

WELLINGTON

QUEEN'S

RD

1

GOUGH

SHING WONG ST

SHANGHAI
LANE

RONIN

ON WO LANE

THE
CHAIRMAN

KAU U

FONG WEST

KAU U FONG

WING KUT ST

7-Eleven

GOUGH
STREET

HOMELESS

KAU
KEE

TIMOTHY
OULTON

HARMAY

SHIN HING ST

OKURA

MARCO
VISCONTI

PETIT
BAZAAR

RYDER
DIAMONDS

WINE
CELLAR

PROLOGUE

HOME
ESSENTIALS

2

HOLLYWOOD

MEE LUN ST

SAM KA LANE

GAGE

STAVELEY ST

ST

PMQ

HKTDC
DESIGN
GALLERY

RD

Pak Tsz
Lane
Park

GAGE
STREET

PEEL ST

SOHOFAMA

GRAHAM
STREET

LITTLE
BAO

THE HK
ROOM

7-Eleven

PEEL
STREET

STREET
MARKETS

3

THE OLD
MAN

LA CABANE
WINE BISTRO

ELGIN ST

GUTZLAFF ST

7-Eleven

ABERDEEN

ALEX CROFT
STREET ART

LYNDHURST

G.O.D.

HOLLYWOOD

7-Eleven

GRAHAM ST

RD

4

CHÔM
CHÔM

PEEL ST

ELGIN ST

STAUNTON ST

A   B   C

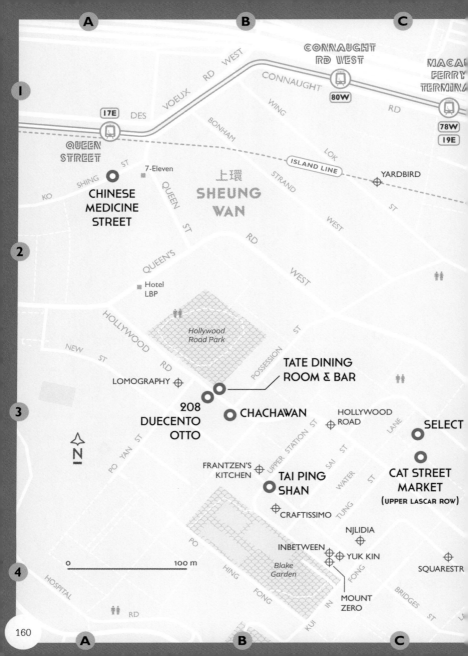

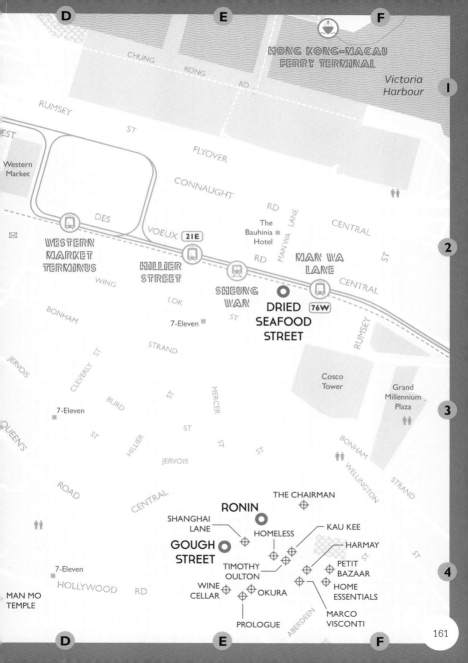

CHUNG KONG RD

HONG KONG–MACAU FERRY TERMINAL

Victoria Harbour

RUMSEY ST

FLYOVER

West

Western Market

CONNAUGHT

DES VOEUX 21E

RD

MAN WA LANE

The Bauhinia Hotel

CENTRAL

WESTERN MARKET TERMINUS

HILLIER STREET

WING

LOK ST

SHEUNG WAN

DRIED SEAFOOD STREET 76W

MAN WA LANE

CENTRAL ST

BONHAM

7-Eleven

STRAND

RUMSEY

JERVOIS

CLEVERLY ST

BURD

ST

MERCER ST

Cosco Tower

Grand Millennium Plaza

7-Eleven

QUEEN'S

ST

HILLIER

JERVOIS

ST

BONHAM

WELLINGTON

STRAND

ROAD

CENTRAL

THE CHAIRMAN

RONIN

SHANGHAI LANE

HOMELESS

KAU KEE

GOUGH STREET

HARMAY

7-Eleven

HOLLYWOOD RD

TIMOTHY OULTON

PETIT BAZAAR

MAN MO TEMPLE

WINE CELLAR

OKURA

HOME ESSENTIALS

PROLOGUE

ABERDEEN

MARCO VISCONTI

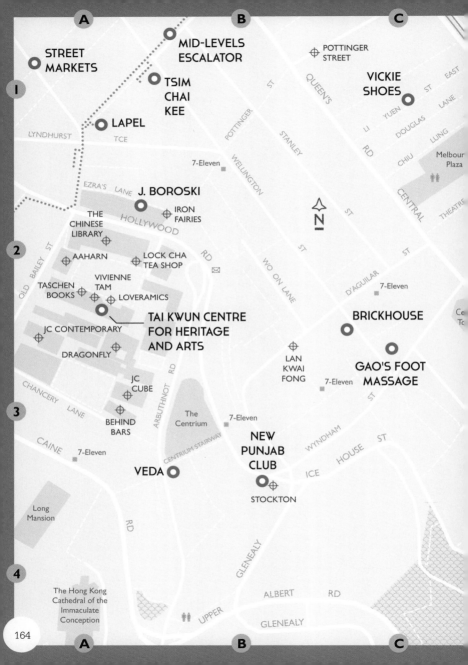

STREET MARKETS

MID-LEVELS ESCALATOR

POTTINGER STREET

VICKIE SHOES

TSIM CHAI KEE

LAPEL

LYNDHURST TCE

7-Eleven

J. BOROSKI

IRON FAIRIES

THE CHINESE LIBRARY

AAHARN

LOCK CHA TEA SHOP

TASCHEN BOOKS

VIVIENNE TAM

LOVERAMICS

TAI KWUN CENTRE FOR HERITAGE AND ARTS

JC CONTEMPORARY

DRAGONFLY

BRICKHOUSE

GAO'S FOOT MASSAGE

LAN KWAI FONG

7-Eleven

JC CUBE

The Centrium

7-Eleven

BEHIND BARS

NEW PUNJAB CLUB

VEDA

STOCKTON

Long Mansion

7-Eleven

CAINE

The Hong Kong Cathedral of the Immaculate Conception

ALBERT RD

GLENEALY

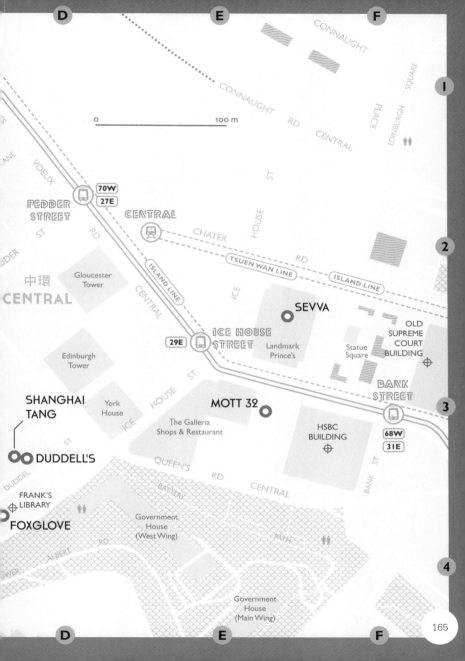

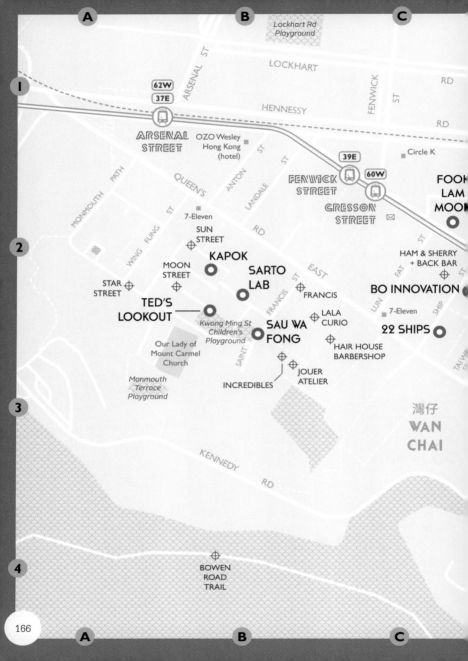

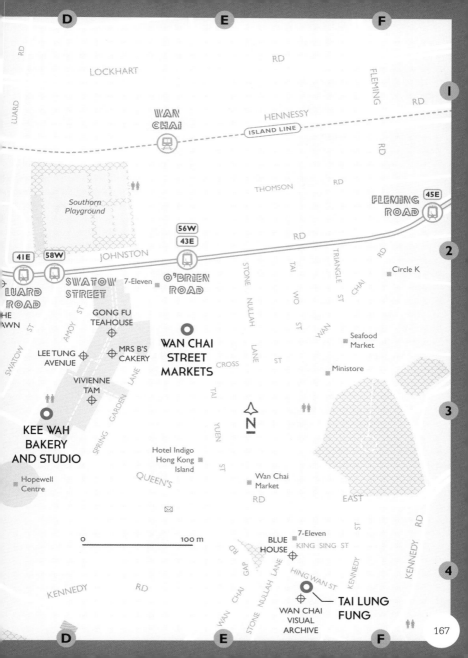

RD

LOCKHART   RD

LUARD

FLEMING

RD

WAN CHAI

HENNESSY

ISLAND LINE

RD

Southorn Playground

THOMSON   RD

FLEMING ROAD   45E

56W
43E   RD

41E   58W
JOHNSTON

LUARD ROAD   SWATOW STREET   7-Eleven   O'BRIEN ROAD

STONE   TAI   TRIANGLE   RD   Circle K
NULLAH   WO   ST

HE AWN

ST

AMOY   GONG FU TEAHOUSE

SWATOW   ST

LEE TUNG AVENUE   MRS B'S CAKERY

VIVIENNE TAM

WAN CHAI STREET MARKETS

LANE   ST

CROSS

SPRING GARDEN LANE

Seafood Market

Ministore

TAI   WAN   ST

3

KEE WAH BAKERY AND STUDIO

YUEN

Hopewell Centre

Hotel Indigo Hong Kong Island

QUEEN'S

ST

Wan Chai Market

RD   EAST

100 m

BLUE HOUSE   7-Eleven   KING SING ST   ST   RD   KENNEDY

HING WAN ST   KENNEDY

WAN CHAI GAP   RD

STONE NULLAH LANE

KENNEDY   RD

TAI LUNG FUNG

WAN CHAI VISUAL ARCHIVE

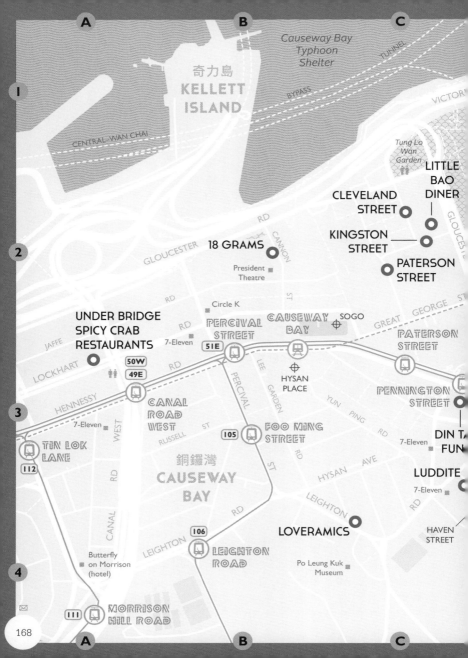

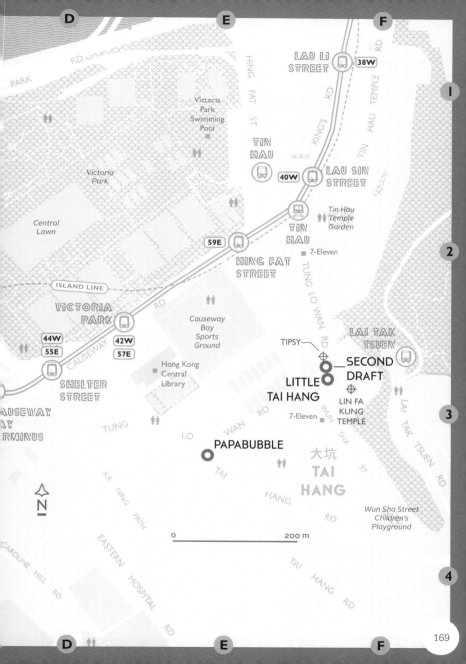

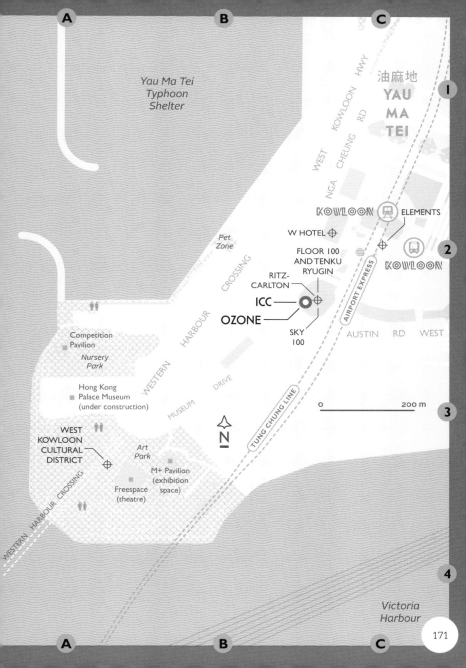

A B C

Yau Ma Tei Typhoon Shelter

1

油麻地
YAU
MA
TEI

WEST KOWLOON HWY

NGA CHEUNG RD

KOWLOON 🚇 ⊕ ELEMENTS

W HOTEL ⊕

FLOOR 100 AND TENKU RYUGIN

RITZ-CARLTON

ICC ⊕ ⊕ 🚇 KOWLOON 2

OZONE

SKY 100

AUSTIN RD WEST

Pet Zone

HARBOUR CROSSING

AIRPORT EXPRESS

WESTERN

■ Competition Pavilion

Nursery Park

■ Hong Kong Palace Museum (under construction)

MUSEUM DRIVE

TUNG CHUNG LINE

0   200 m

3

WEST KOWLOON CULTURAL DISTRICT ⊕

Art Park

N

■ M+ Pavilion (exhibition space)

■ Freespace (theatre)

WESTERN HARBOUR CROSSING

4

Victoria Harbour

A B C

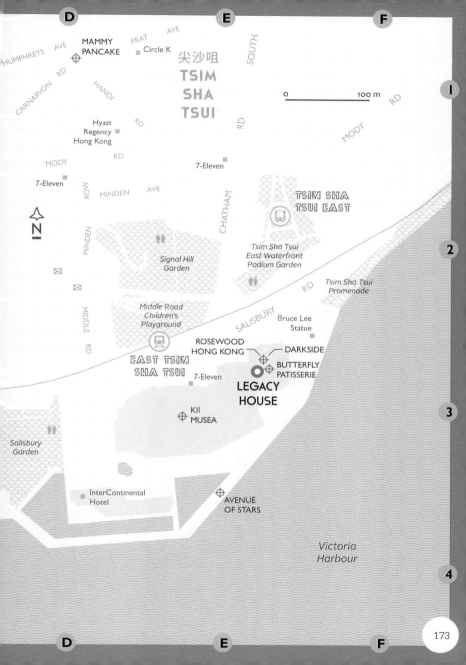

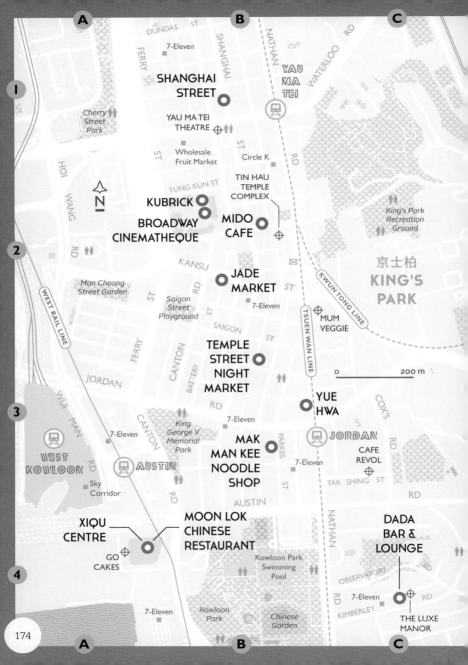

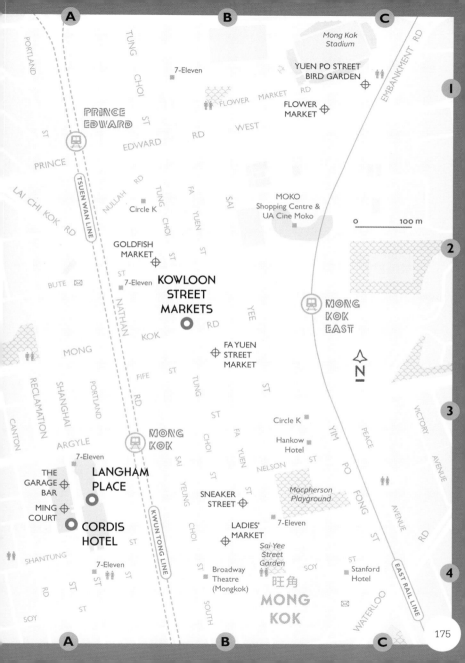

A

B

C

I

TSUEN WAN LINE

VINYL HERO

KOWLOON RESTAURANT

7-Eleven

7-Eleven

HOP YICK TAI

LEUNG TIM CHOPPERS FACTORY

A1 TOFU COMPANY

7-Eleven

APLIU STREET

CHOW

KI

YU

CHAU

ST

LAI

2

FABRIC STREET
(YEN CHOW ST HAWKER BAZAAR)

7-Eleven

TAI

ST

LUNG

KI LUNG STREET

CHI

KWEILIN

NAN

SAN LUNG CAKE SHOP

ST

YEN

N

YEE

KOK

PEI HO STREET

深水埗
SHAM SHUI PO

HAI

3

TUNG

KUK

ST

7-Eleven

RD

ST

ST

TAN

HO

CHEONG

WEST

CHAU

PEI

ST

0   100 m

Tung Chau Street Park

KOWLOON

ST

NAM

4

CHEONG

SAN

Squash Centre

CORRIDOR

Cheong Yin House

LANE

A

B

C

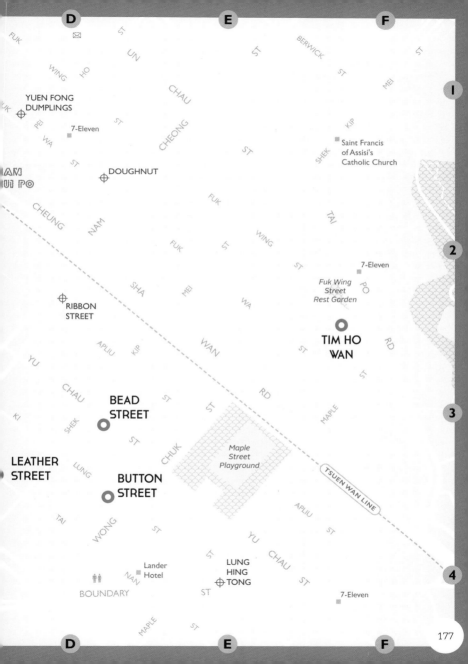

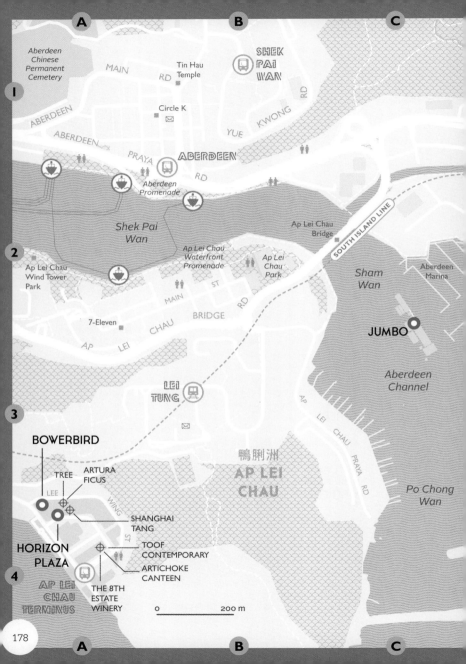

Aberdeen Chinese Permanent Cemetery

MAIN

RD

Tin Hau Temple

Circle K

ABERDEEN

ABERDEEN

PRAYA

ABERDEEN

RD

YUE

KWONG

RD

SHEK PAI WAN

Aberdeen Promenade

Shek Pai Wan

Ap Lei Chau Bridge

SOUTH ISLAND LINE

Sham Wan

Aberdeen Marina

Ap Lei Chau Wind Tower Park

Ap Lei Chau Waterfront Promenade

Ap Lei Chau Park

7-Eleven

MAIN

ST

CHAU

BRIDGE

RD

JUMBO

AP

LEI

Aberdeen Channel

LEI TUNG

鴨脷洲
AP LEI CHAU

AP

LEI

CHAU

PRAYA

RD

Po Chong Wan

BOWERBIRD

TREE

ARTURA FICUS

LEE

WING

SHANGHAI TANG

HORIZON PLAZA

TOOF CONTEMPORARY

ST

ARTICHOKE CANTEEN

AP LEI CHAU TERMINUS

THE 8TH ESTATE WINERY

0   200 m

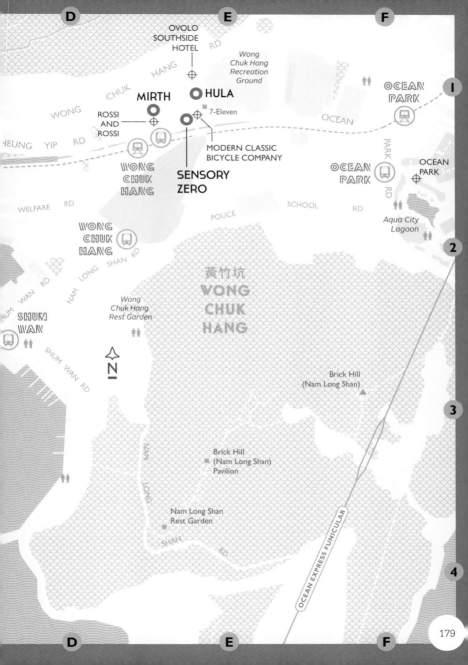

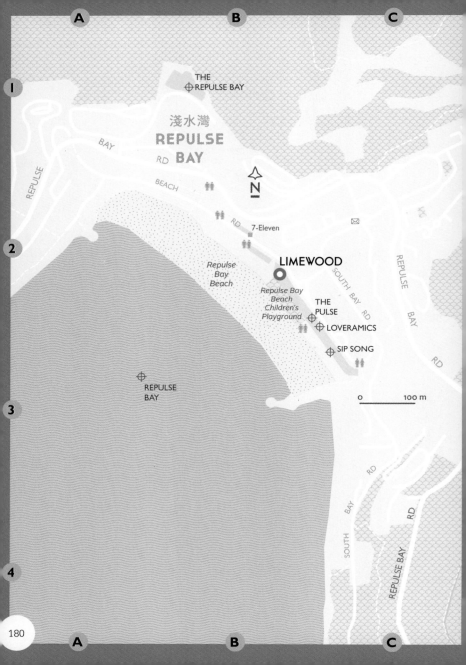

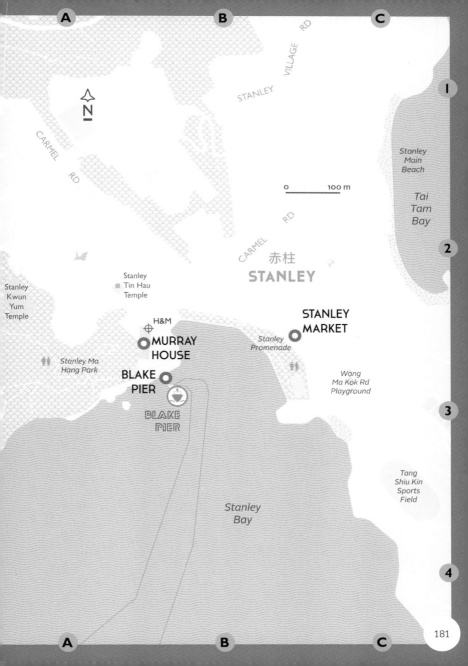

INDEX

8th Estate Winery, The 85
18 Grams 59, 168 B2
22 Ships 42–3, 166 C3
208 Duecento Otto 75, 160 B3
1881 Heritage 98

A1 Tofu Company 127, 176 B2
Adrenalin 50
Ah Por Tofu Fa 141
Ahaarn 26
Airport Express 150
Albergue 1601 132
Albergue da Santa Casa da Misericòlrdia 131
Antoìnio 135
Apliu Street 120
Aqua Luna 80, 95, 163 F3, 172 B3
Artichoke Canteen 85
Artura Ficus 85
Avenue of Stars 94

Baccarat 98
Bathers 149
beaches, Lantau Island 149
Bead Street (Yu Chau St) 122
Behind Bars 26
Big Wave Bay 81
Blake Pier 80, 181 B3
Blue House heritage building 47
Bluebell 85
Bo Innovation 44, 166 C2
Bookworm 140
Bowen Road Trail 58
Bowerbird 84, 85, 178 A4
Brickhouse vii, 16–17, 164 C3
Broadway Cinematheque 108, 174 B2
Butterfly Patisserie 101
Button Street (Ki Lung St) 122

Cafe Revol 116
Cat Street Market (Upper Lascar Row) vii, 67, 160 C3

Causeway Bay 48–63
Central xii–23
Chachawan 74, 160 B3
Chairman, The 73
Chapel of St Francis Xavier 136
Chinese Library for Cantonese 26
Chinese Medicine Street vii, 66, 160 A2
Chloe 85
Chôm Chôm 30, 158 B4
Cleveland Street 54–5, 168 B3
Coloane village 136
Cordis Hotel 113
Cotai strip (casino area) 133
Craftissimo vii, 70
Cunha Bazaar 134

Dada Bar + Lounge 105, 174 C4
DarkSide bar 101
Des Voeux Road West vii
Diesel 85
Dim Sum 58, 170 C3
Din Tai Fung 61, 168 C3
Doughnut backpacks 122
Dragonfly 26
Dragon's Back Trail 81, 157 E4
Dried Seafood Street vii, 66, 161 E2
Duddell's vii, 20–1, 165 D3

Eduardo Marques Square 136
8th Estate Winery, The 85
18 Grams 59, 168 B2
1881 Heritage 98
Elements mall 99
Ermenegildo Zegna 85

Fa Yuen Street Market 111, 175 B3
Fabric Street (Yen Chow St – Hawker Bazaar) 122, 176 A2
Family Trail Walk, Lamma Island 141
Felix 98
Floor 101 99
Flower Market 111, 175 C1
Fong Kei 134
Fook Lam Moon 45, 166 C2
Four Seasons Hotel 76, 77

Foxglove vii, 19, 165 D4
Francis 38
Frank's Library 19
Frantzen's Kitchen vii, 70

Gage Street 5
Gao's Foot Massage vii, 6, 164 C3
Garage Bar, The 113, 175 A3
Go Cakes 96
G.O.D. vii, 29, 158 B4
Goldfish Market 111, 175 B2
Gong Fu Tea 40
Gough Street vii, 69, 158 A2, 161 E4
Goughs on Gough 69
Graham Street 5

Hac Sa Beach 137
Hair House Barbershop 39
Ham & Sherry 43
Happy Valley 3, 48–63
Happy Valley Races 50–1, 170 B2
Harmay 69
Haven Street 56
heritage trams vii, 2–3, 151
HK Room, The 28
HKTDC Design Gallery 28
Hollywood Rd vii
Home Essentials 69
Homeless 69
Hong Kong Cultural Centre 98
Hong Kong Foodie Tours 114
Hong Kong–Guangzhou train 151
Hong Kong International Airport 99, 146, 150
Hong Kong Island South 78–91
Hong Kong Museum of Art 98
Hong Kong Park 19
Hong Kong trams vii, 2–3, 151
Hong Kong–Zhuhai–Macau bridge 146, 151
Hop Yick Tai 124, 176 C2
Horizon Plaza 85, 178 A4
HSBC Building 18
Hugo Boss 85
Hula 84, 179 E1
Hung Shing Yeh Beach 141
Hysan Place 54

ICC 99, 171 C2
IFC shopping mall 77
in-town check-in service for Hong Kong International Airport passengers 99, 150
InBetween vii, 70
Incredibles 39
Iron Fairies 33

J. Boroski 33, 159 D4, 164 A2
Jade Market 110, 174 B2
JC Contemporary 26
JC Cube 26
Jimmy Chen 98
Jordan 106–17
Jouer Atelier 39
Joyce 85
Juice Couture 85
Jumbo 88–9, 178 C2

K11 Musea 101
Kapok 37, 166 B2
Kate Spade New York 85
Kau Kee 69
Kee Wah Bakery and Studio 40–1, 167 D3
Kent & Curwean 98
Ki Lung Street (Button Street) 120, 177 D3
Kingston Street 54–5, 168 B3
Kowloon Restaurant 125, 176 B1
Kowloon Street Markets 111
Kubrick 108, 174 B2

La Cabane Wine Bistro 31, 158 B3
Ladies' Market 111, 175 B4
Lala Curio 95
Lamma Fisherfolk's Village 141
Lamma Island 138–43
Lan Kwai Fong vii
Lane Crawford 85
Langham Place 113
Lantau Island 144–9
Lapel vii, 7, 158 C3, 164 A1
Leather Street (Tai Nan St) 122, 177 D3
Leung Tim Choppers Factory 121
Limewood 90–1, 180 B2
Lin Fa KungTemple 57

Little Bao Diner 62–3, 168 B3
Little Tai Hang 168 C6
Lobby, The 98
Lock Cha Tea Shop 26
Lomography 70
Long Wa Teahouse 130
Lord Stow's Bakery 136
Loveramics 53, 169 D3
Lower Cheung Sha Beach 149
Luddite 56, 168 C3
Lung Hing Tong 125
Lung King Heen 76–7, 162 B3

Macau 128–37
Macau Ferries 151
Main Shrine Hall of Buddha 147
Mak Man Kee Noodle Shop 117, 174 B3
Mammy Pancake 96
Man Mo Temple vii, 67
Marco Visconti 69
Market streets, Sham Shui Po 120–1
Mercearia Portuguesa 131
Mid-Levels Escalator vii, 4, 151, 162 A3, 164 B1
Mido Café 116, 174 B2
Ming Court 113, 175 A4
Mirth 83, 179 E1
Mok Yee Kei 134
Mong Kok 106–17
Monocle 98
Moon Lok Chinese Restaurant 102–3, 174 A4
Moon Street 46
Mott 32 14–15, 165 E3
Mount Zero vii, 70
Mrs B's Cakery 40
Mum Veggie 108
Murray House 80, 181 B3

Nei Lak Shan Country Trail, Lantau Island 147
New Punjab Club 22–3, 164 B4
Ngong Ping 360 Cable Car 146
Njlidia 70

Ocean Park 84
Okura 69
Old Man, The 32, 158 A3
Old Supreme Court 18
Old Taipa Village 135

Old Tin Ha Temple 136
OZONE 99, 104, 171 C2

Papabubble 52, 168 C5
Para Site 70
Paterson Street 54–5, 168 B3
Pawn, The 44
Peak, The 2, 68
Peak Tram 21, 68, 151
Peel Street 5
Pei Ho Street 120
Peninsula, The 98, 172 C3
Petit Bazaar 69
Piaget 98
pink dolphin tours 148
PMQ vii, 28, 158 A3
Po Lin Monastery 146, 147
Pottinger Street 5
Prince Edward 106–17
Prologue 69
Pui O Beach 149

Qi – Nine Dragons 100, 172 C2

Rainbow Seafood Restaurant 142
Repulse Bay 78, 90
Restaurante Fernando 137
Ribbon Street (Nam Cheong St) 122
Riquexo 133
Ritz-Carlton 99
Ronin 73, 158 B1, 161 E4
Rosewood Hong Kong Hotel 101
Rossi and Rossi 86
Rua da Felicidade 130
Ruins of St Pauls 132

Sai Ying Pun 72
St Lazarus neighbourhood 131
Sampan Seafood Restaurant 140
San Lung Cake Shop 127
Sanreve 70
Sarto Lab 38, 166 B2
Sau Wa Fong 39, 166 B3
Second Draft 57, 63, 168 C6
Select 18 68, 160 C3
Sensory Zero 87, 179 E1
Sevva 18, 165 E2
Sham Shui Po 118–27
Shanghai Lane 69
Shanghai Street 109, 174 B1

Shanghai Tang vii, 8, 85, 165 D3
Shek O 81
Sheung Wan 64–77
Shiatzy Chen 98
Silvermine Bay Beach 149
Sip Song 90
Sky100 99
Sneaker Street 111, 175 B4
Sogo 54
Soho 24–33
Sohofama 28
Sok Kwu Wan Seafood Restaurant Street 142–3
Sok Kwu Wan village 141
Spring Moon 98
Squarestreet vii, 70
Stanley Dragon Boat Races 82
Stanley Market 82, 181 B3
Star Ferries 94, 150–1, 172 A3
Stockton 22
Street Markets vii, 5, 111, 158 C3, 164 A1
Sun Hing Street 46
Sun Street 46
Symphony of Lights 94

Tai Hang 48–63
Tai Hang Fire Dragon Dance 52
Tai Kwun Centre for Heritage and Arts vii, 13, 26–7, 53, 164 A2
Tai Lung Fung 47, 167 F4
Tai Nan Street (Leather Street) 122, 177 D3
Tai O 148
Tai O Heritage Hotel 148
Tai Ping Shan vii, 70–1, 160 B3
Taschem Books 26
Tate Dining Room & Bar 72, 160 B3
Ted's Lookout 46, 166 B2
Temple Street Night Foodie Tour 114
Temple Street Night Market 114–15, 174 B3
Tenku RyuGin 99
The 8th Estate Winery 85
The Chairman 73
The Garage Bar 113, 175 A4
The HK Room 28
The Legacy House 101, 173 E3

The Lobby 98
The Old Man 32, 158 A3
The Pawn 44
The Peak 2, 68
The Peninsula 98, 172 C3
Tian Tan Buddha 146, 147
Tim Ho Wan 126, 177 F2
Timothy Oulton 69
Tin Hau Temple, Lamma Island 140
Tin Hau Temple Complex, Yau Ma Tei 110
Tipsy 57
Toof Contemporary 85
Tree 85
Tsim Chai Kee vii, 10, 159 D3, 164 A1
Tsim Sha Tsui 92–105
22 Ships 42–3, 166 C3
208 Duecento Otto 75, 160 B3

Under Bridge Spicy Crab Restaurants 61, 168 C1

Veda 12, 164 B3
Vickie Shoes vii, 9, 159 F3, 164 C1
Vinyl Hero 123, 176 C1
Vivienne Tam 26, 40

Wan Chai 34–47
Wan Chai Street Markets 36, 167 E2
Wan Chai Visual Archive art space 47
West Kowloon 92–105
Wine Cellar 31
Wing Lok St vii
Wong Chuk Hang's Modern Classic Bicycle Company 89

Xiqu Centre 96–7, 174 A4

Yardbird 66
Yau Ma Tei 106–17
Yau Ma Tei Theatre 109
Yu Chau Street (Bead Street) 177 D3
Yue Hwa 112, 174 B3
Yuen Fong Dunplings 126
Yuen Po Street Bird Market and Garden 111, 175 C1
Yuk Kin 70
Yung Shue Wan Village 140

ABOUT THE AUTHOR

Award-winning writer, journalist and author Penny Watson has travelled the world, written feature articles for countless magazines and newspapers, and researched a number of guidebooks, including *Hong Kong Precincts* (2015), *London Pocket Precincts* (2019) and *Slow Travel* (2019). She is currently working on *Ultimate Campsites: Australia*. Penny lived in Hong Kong for six years and returns two or three times each year. The city has become one of her niche writing topics – when she returns it still feels like home. She is a member of both the British Guild of Travel Writers and Australian Society of Travel Writers. She currently resides in Melbourne with her partner Pippy and their two children Digby and Etienne.

ACKNOWLEDGEMENT*S*

Big thanks to the Hardie Grant team for publishing my fourth solo book. And especially to editors Megan Cuthbert and Alice Barker for pulling it all together, and publisher Melissa Kayser who commissioned this book and its predecessor *Hong Kong Precincts*.

Hong Kong Pocket Precincts was largely written in Melbourne coffee shops after returning from research stints in Hong Kong. Within days of my final trip, the protests had kicked off in Hong Kong. I hope, by the time this book goes to print, the political environment has settled, the people retain their liberties, and the city remains the peaceful place I know it to be.

Lastly, thanks to my family. My relationship with Hong Kong will forever be tied to my partner Pipster. We arrived in Hong Kong with backpacks as a newly married couple and left six years later with three-year-old Digby, Eti on the way, a container of furniture and a lifetime's worth of memories. The experience has shaped our little family in so many ways and will continue to do so.

PHOTO CREDITS

All images are © Penny Watson except for the following contributed images:

Hong Kong Tourism Board p. 2–3, 4, 18, 36, 94, 95, 96, 114, 116, 123, 146, 147, 149; Shanghai Tang p. 8; Veda p. 12; Mott32 pp. 14–15; Brickhouse p. 16–17; Foxglove p. 19; Duddells pp. 20–21; New Punjab Club pp. 22–23; Shutterstock p. 27 (middle and bottom right), 111; Chom Chom p. 30; La Cabane p. 21; The Old Man p. 32; 22 Ships pp. 42–43; Bo Innovation p. 44; Fook Lam Moon p. 45; Happy Valley Races p. 50–51; Din Tai Fung p. 60; Little Bao Diner p.. 62–63; Tate Dining p. 72; Jason Michael Lang p. 73; Chachawan p. 74; 208 Duecento Otto p. 75; Lung King Heen pp. 76–77; Joe Chen p. 81; Jumbo 88–89; Limewood pp. 90–91; Peninsula p. 98; ICC p. 99; Ozone p. 104; Dada Bar p. 105; Langham Place p. 113; iStock p. 115, 129; Vincent Sin 132; Forbes Conrad p. 136.

ARCHITECTURE

Xiqu Centre, Tsim Sha Tsui & West Kowloon … 96

Tai Kwun Centre for Heritage and Arts, Soho … 26

The Peninsula, Tsim Sha Tsui & West Kowloon … 98

Man Mo Temple, Sheung Wan … 67

HSBC Building, Central … 18

Old Supreme Court building, Central … 18

DIM /UM

Mott 32, Central … 14

Duddell's, Central … 20

Dim Sum, Causeway Bay, Happy Valley & Tai Hung … 58

Moon Lok Chinese Restaurant, Tsim Sha Tsui & West Kowloon … 102

Shanghai Lane, Sheung Wan …

Din Tai Fung, Causeway Bay, Happy Valley & Tai Hung … 49

Lung King Heen, Sheung Wan … 76

/ECRET BAR/

Foxglove, Central … 19

Brickhouse, Central … 16

Stockton, Central … 22

J. Boroski, Soho … 33

Back Bar and Ham & Sherry, Wan Chai … 43

CHEAP EAT/ HONG KONG I/LAND

Tsim Chai Kee, Central … 11

Little Bao Diner, Causeway Bay, Happy Valley & Tai Hung … 62

Shanghai Lane, Sheung Wan … 69

Kau Kee, Gough Street, Sheung Wan … 69

Yuk Kin, Tai Ping Shan, Sheung Wan … 70

CHEAP EAT/ KOWLOON-/IDE

Mak Man Kee Noodle Shop, Jordan & Beyond … 117

Temple Street Night Market, Jordan & Beyond … 114

Mido Cafe, Jordan & Beyond … 116

Hop Yick Tai, Sham Shui Po … 124

Kowloon Restaurant, Sham Shui Po … 125

Tim Ho Wan, Sham Shui Po … 126

A1 Tofu Company, Sham Shui Po … 127

A PERFECT HONG KONG DAY

My perfect days in Hong Kong are many and varied. You'll need decent walking shoes for this one. Start early wandering around Central's evocative **Street Markets**, where vendors sell flapping fish and crustaceans, 100-year-old eggs and fresh Asian greens. Meander downhill to **Tsim Chai Kee** for a cheap and delicious bowl of wonton and noodle soup for breakfast. Shops start to open at 10.30am. Find your way to **Vickie Shoes** for made-to-measure shoes, **Shanghai Tang** for pricey-but-nicey Hong Kong gifts and **Lapel** for tailored work shirts (all the while taking in towering buildings, flashy big-brand shops and busy street life). Take the outdoor **Mid-Levels Escalator** for the novelty, and because the hill is too steep to walk, to **Tai Kwun Centre for Heritage and Arts**, where shops, eateries, hip bars and art galleries populate a cluster of inspiring architecture. Exit onto **Hollywood Road** and turn west to walk along Hong Kong's oldest street. Stop in at iconic Hong Kong gift shop **G.O.D.** and, on the wall outside, see the city's most recognisable street art. Detour uphill at Aberdeen Street to **PMQ**, a hub for creatives, and downhill via Shin Hing for a peek at **Gough Street's** indie shops. Continue walking along Hollywood Road to beautiful **Man Mo Temple**. Across the road, **Cat Street Market (Upper Lascar Row)** has hawker stalls selling ancient-looking snuff bottles, Mao cigarette lighters and jade-esque bangles. Real antiques – the Ming vase variety – can be found in gallery-style stores at this end of Hollywood Road. Head to Scandinavian design store **Square Street** for a decent latte, then wind your way up to **Tai Ping Shan**, a quietly cool street of cute street-level shops. Go Nordic for lunch at **Frantzen's Kitchen**, and enjoy a craft beer outside **Craftissimo** before popping by **InBetween** for vintage collectibles and **Mount Zero** for books. Navigate to **Wing Lok Street** and **Des Voeux Road West** to lock eyes on the **Chinese Medicine** and **Dried Seafood shops** before jumping on one of the quaint two-storey **heritage trams** back to Central. The steep walk to **Lan Kwai Fong** can be rewarded with a reflexology foot massage at **Gao's Foot Massage**. The rooftop at **Duddell's** is perfect for a cheeky sundowner – and a Cantonese fine-dining dinner – or go to **Brickhouse** for a cheaper Mexican feast. Finish the day with a jazz session at **Foxglove**, one of the city's intriguing hidden venues.

CONTENTS

Introduction … v
A perfect Hong Kong day … vii
Pocket top picks … viii
Hong Kong overview map … x

Precincts
Central … xii
Soho … 24
Wan Chai … 34
Causeway Bay, Happy Valley & Tai Hang … 48
Sheung Wan … 64
Hong Kong Island South … 78
Tsim Sha Tsui & West Kowloon … 92
Jordan & Beyond … 106
Sham Shui Po … 118

Field trips
Macau … 128
Lamma Island … 138
Lantau Island … 144

Travel tips … 150
Maps … 156
Index … 182
About the author & acknowledgements … 184
Photo credits … 185

INTRODUCTION

Hong Kong is one of the coolest cities in the world to travel to. In my six years as a resident, and on oodles of visits since, I've narrowed its appeal down to two things – its extreme contrasts and its constant contradictions.

To witness the East-meets-West fusion of this former British colony, walk past colonial churches alongside Buddhist shrines and choose between traditional teahouses and barista-run cafes. To glimpse its rich-versus-poor shops, head to a sky-high big-brand shopping mall before having a streetside bowl of Mom and Pop noodles. To see how rural traditions still hold fast against economic development, travel from the heckle of high-rises to remote islands where village life remains unchanged. This is Hong Kong – a vibrant, often chaotic, and exciting place that captures your heart with its lust for life.

In *Hong Kong Pocket Precincts*, I have tapped into cultural hangouts, sights and activities, shops, bars and eateries that show this multi-faceted personality.

On Hong Kong Island's northside, I take you to five-star eateries serving pork buns in silver baskets and hidden bars serving bespoke cocktails, as well as to a local dried seafood market, on a heritage tram ride and to have a reflexology foot massage.

The southside is all about beachside Repulse Bay and the wilderness on the Dragon's Back Trail, but also Wong Chuck Hang's unique galleries and retail outlets in horizontal industrial warehouses.

Across Victoria Harbour, Tsim Sha Tsui and West Kowloon are changing fast, with the beginnings of the West Kowloon Cultural District leading the way. Beyond, Kowloon's Nathan Road is a hot spot to discover Eastern traditions with street markets, down-to-earth dumpling shops and authentic tofu stalls.

The Field Trip chapters inspire daytrips to the islands of Lantau and Lamma to explore famous sights set against parkland and mountain peaks, and to Macau, a city only an hour away by ferry, but a world away in terms of its unique Portuguese–Cantonese culture.

If you fall for somewhere I've recommended, let me know. If this book helps you find your own gem, share the love at: pennywatson.com.au; Instagram watson_penny.

Penny Watson